M000317643

Socially AWKWARD

Pressing Through Discomfort to Engage Tough Topics

Ruth Buchanan

E

Socially Awkward
© Copyright 2021 Ruth Buchanan

ISBN: 978-1-944120-99-3

Unless otherwise noted, all scriptures are taken from *The Holy Bible*, English Standard Version® (ESV®), copyright © 2001 by Crossway, a publishing ministry of Good News Publishers. Used by permission. All rights reserved.

Scriptures marked CSB are from *The Holy Bible*, the Christian Standard Bible. Copyright © 2017 by Holman Bible Publishers.

Scriptures marked KJV are from *The Holy Bible*, the Authorized (King James) Version.

Scriptures marked NASB are from *The Holy Bible*, New American Standard Bible. Copyright © 1960, 1962, 1963, 1968, 1971, 1972, 1973, 1975, 1977, 1995 by The Lockman Foundation.

Scriptures marked NIV are from *The Holy Bible, New International Version®*, copyright © 1973, 1978, 1984, 2011 by Biblical, Inc.™ Used by permission of Zondervan. All rights reserved worldwide. www.zondervan.com.

Scriptures marked NKJV are from *The Holy Bible*, the New King James Version®. Copyright © 1982 by Thomas Nelson. Used by permission. All rights reserved.

Scriptures marked NLT are from *The Holy Bible*, New Living Translation. Copyright ©1996, 2004, 2015 by Tyndale House Foundation.

All rights reserved. No part of this publication may be reproduced or transmitted in any form or by any means without written permission from the publisher.

Published by:

 Entrusted Books, an imprint of Write Integrity Press
PO Box 702852; Dallas, TX 75370
www.WriteIntegrity.com

Published in the United States of America

For those who trip
and fall
and get back up
and trip again
while everyone's still looking . . .

You are my people.
This book is for us.

CONTENTS

Author's Note 7

Welcome to Awkwardsville: The Time I Made the Tozer Joke 9

Chapter 1: Let's Get Awkward 13

Welcome to Awkwardsville: Private Showing 25

Chapter 2: Willing to Go There 29

Welcome to Awkwardsville: The Time I Stopped Soccer Practice 47

Chapter 3: Anything but Black and White 51

Welcome to Awkwardsville: Now Accepting Compliments 79

Chapter 4: Let's Talk About Sex 81

Welcome to Awkwardsville: The Kicker 101

Chapter 5: Bearing the Weight 103

Welcome to Awkwardsville: Awkward in Auckland 121

Chapter 6: Call Me Crazy 123

Welcome to Awkwardsville: Whispering Hope 139

Chapter 7: No Middle Ground 143

Welcome to Awkwardsville: At the Tips of My Fingers 157

Chapter 8: Of Such Is the Kingdom 161

Welcome to Awkwardsville: Exercise in Humility 173

Chapter 9: When We Are Weak 177

Welcome to Awkwardsville: The Not-Date 193

Chapter 10: Day of the Dead 197

Welcome to Awkwardsville: "I'll be right over there." 209

Chapter 11: Who Hurt You? 213

Welcome to Awkwardsville: When You Need to Go 235

Chapter 12: Pressing Forward 239

Acknowledgments 247

About the Author 248

AUTHOR'S NOTE

Occasionally during this book, I have changed the names and identifying characteristics of certain people to protect their privacy, either at their direct request or by exercising my own judgment. My intent is not to deceive but to provide context for the discussion while still preserving the dignity of those who have trusted me with their stories over the years. Thank you.

Lord, make me willing to be awkward for you.

Welcome to Awkwardsville:
The Time I Made the Tozer Joke

Some situations are so embarrassing there's simply no sensible way to recover.

A few winters ago, I flew north to visit my friend Joanna for a week. We'd driven across town to pick up her then-school-aged daughter from a birthday party at the home of people who were friends with Joanna but strangers to me.

"You're going to love this house," Joanna said. "If they don't offer us a tour, try to get a look around anyway." So, while she chatted with the mother of the birthday girl, I craned my neck, glancing down hallways and up staircases, trying to get a good idea of the floorplan.

That's when I spied it.

The Bookcase.

Tucked under a polished wooden staircase, this bookcase had its own internal lighting system and looked hermetically sealed. Behind tight glass panels were displayed a wide array of first edition and out-of-print books.

I don't remember walking over, but I must have done so,

because there I was. Perhaps I levitated. Angel choirs sang as I drew near. Too near. I likely left a nose print on the glass. My fingers itched to open the panels and caress those soft spines.

But no. I was a guest. Not even a guest. A tag-along.

Speaking of which, perhaps I was rude to wander off by myself without even an introduction. I hustled to the kitchen, where Joanna stood chatting with the homeowner. Their conversation broke as I approached, and some men (dads of the partygoers, I assumed) returned from outside to join us.

"You've got a great collection of books," I said, gesturing toward The Bookcase.

The wife smiled as a man I took to be her husband joined our little circle. "This guy just loves old books," she gushed. "In the early days of the internet, when he realized he could buy them for a steal, he went online and just snapped them all up. Really cheap, too. Some of them are even signed by the authors."

I thought of a first edition Tolkien I'd spied, and my brain softened around the edges. But everyone was staring at me. I should say something.

"You must really like Tozer." I referenced an entire row of A.W. Tozer's early works I'd spied nestled on those shelves, many of them identical copies.

"Oh." The wife brightened. "Do you know Tozer?"

"Well," I deadpanned, "not personally."

A flat silence ensued, broken only by shrieking of the children upstairs and the sound of a half-muffled snort from Joanna. Bless her. She always laughs at my jokes, good or otherwise. Judging by the way the rest of the group was staring at me, this must have been otherwise.

Then the wife smiled kindly. She tilted her head to the side and leaned in. I detected soft pity in her expression. "Oh, honey," she tutted. "Tozer's dead."

Her husband nodded slowly, regarding me seriously through his glasses. "Tozer was part of the Christian and Missionary Alliance Movement." He adopted a tone halfway between tour guide and high school principal. "He was a really well-known preacher and writer. His best-known work is probably *The Pursuit of God.*"

"Well," I fumbled, trying to think how to backpedal gracefully. "I know who Tozer is. I mean, I know he's dead." Even to my own ears, I sounded defensive.

I wasn't lying, though. I have a master's degree in theological studies. I've read Tozer extensively, partly due to my education and partially due to the influence of a favorite professor who had studied directly under Tozer back in the day. (Way back in the day.) I certainly knew Tozer. But it was hard to figure out how to say all this without sounding pompous, which—I've been told—I have a tendency to do.

Someone changed the subject.

Joanna wound up the chat and collected her daughter. The minute we were back in the car, she turned to face me. "That," she said, "was awesome."

I drooped in the passenger's seat, turning up my coat collar against my freezing neck. "I don't want to talk about it."

She shifted into drive. "Well, if it's any consolation, I thought it was funny."

"What's wrong with me?" I asked, and not for the first time. Why couldn't I just have regular conversations?

Joanna glanced in her mirrors and pulled out into the quiet street. "There's nothing wrong with you. But I do have a suggestion."

I was all ears.

"Maybe try not acting like yourself until people have already gotten to know you."

Lifted from the context of our long and loving friendship, her comment may sound harsh, but in that moment, I knew exactly what she meant. We laughed together as she pulled away from the curb, commiserating over the awkwardness of meeting new people. There is a sheer relief in finding friends who put up with us, love us, and challenge us to become the best possible versions of ourselves. For me, these changes have most often come about through awkward conversations.

CHAPTER 1
Let's Get Awkward

As you read earlier, I'm socially awkward. I'm not afraid to admit it because I know I'm in good company. At one point or another, everyone's awkward. We're all out here just bumbling through life, trying to maintain our dignity as best we can. In many cases, the ability to hold on hinges on little moments of shared laughter at humanity, locking eyes and shaking our heads over how extremely taxing it can be sometimes just to be a person.

Between the chapters of this book, in sections marked "Welcome to Awkwardsville," you'll get an inside look at my highlight reel of personal pratfalls. However, the bulk of our focus will be on more serious matters.

Together, we will explore the following questions: Why do so many of us avoid uncomfortable conversations? How does this tendency affect us? Why is it worth it to press through the awkwardness and tackle tough topics? How can we learn to adjust our thinking and seek change? What's at stake if we don't?

Why This Matters

Many of us find ourselves drastically underprepared to talk about uncomfortable topics, even in cases when we acknowledge the importance of the subject matter. Such as having "the talk" with children. You know what I mean. The sex talk.

Though sex and sexuality are two of the most important and universal topics caregivers should discuss with their children, they're all too often avoided, glossed over, or swept under the rug. While over 80% of parents and caregivers consider it important to talk to their children about issues surrounding sex and sexuality— such as abstinence, the consequences and effects of sex, and protection methods—a significantly lower amount (about 60%) actually claim to feel comfortable and confident doing so. If you're surprised by the 20% drop, buckle up. The number who actually follow through is truly dismal.

Only 8% of caregivers admit to discussing sexual health issues with their children "very often." Another 37% claim they do it "sometimes"; 22% report "seldom/hardly ever"; and around 33% say "never."[1] The gap from eighty percent to eight percent shows the difference between good intentions and good choices. And that gap? It has an impact, as we will soon discuss.

Believe me, I get it. Talking about sex is just awkward. Especially with our own kids. As a friend once told me around the time her kids were on the cusp of adolescence, "Once I tell them

---

[1] National Institutes of Health, "Do parents talk to their adolescent children about sex?" https://www.ncbi.nlm.nih.gov/pubmed/22821244 (Accessed November 29, 2019).

about sex, they'll know what my husband and I are doing when our bedroom door is closed, and I don't know if I'm ready for that."

It made me laugh when she said it, but I get where she's coming from. A little girl who'd just learned about sex once asked me point blank why I'd grown breasts if I'd never actually fed a baby. You try answering that one without feeling awkward.

Still, it's truly unfortunate that so many caregivers resist talking with their charges about sex because these talks have a proven quantifiable impact. Forthright talks about sex and sexuality serve to satisfy kids' very natural curiosity while simultaneously impressing on them the seriousness of it all.

According to one 2018 study, "Parents talking about sex with youth does not lead to sexual debut. In fact, adolescents who rate their general communication with parents favorably are less likely to be sexually active. There is strong support that children who received messages to wait for marriage before sex were not as sexually active compared to those who were not given explicit instructions."[2]

In Chapter 4, we'll discuss in greater detail how to talk about sex and sexuality. For now, let's consider this: If talking to children about sex can yield helpful results, is feeling awkward about it a reasonable excuse for putting it off? Furthermore, if parents are skipping the all-important "sex talk," what else are they avoiding?

This isn't just about parents, though. This is about all of us.

---

[2] National Institutes of Health, "21st Century Parent-Child Sex Communication in the U.S.: A Process Review." https://www.ncbi.nlm.nih.gov/pmc/articles/PMC5808426/ (Accessed November 29, 2019).

And it's not just sex. We all have topics we consciously avoid. Why are we avoiding them? Is our silence helpful or harmful? Who's being most affected—and whom are we really trying to protect?

Loving the Wall

In his poem "Mending Wall," American poet Robert Frost tells of two landowners walking their shared property line, literally mending fences. While one neighbor asserts the need of walls ("Good fences make good neighbors"), the other neighbor reasons as to why this is so. Along the way, readers can ponder a deep irony. The wall isn't just something that separates the two landowners. It's also the very thing that has drawn them together that particular day. The whole poem is a metaphor, of course, and if we took the time, we could find plenty of loose threads to pull.[3] For now, let's reflect on this: establishing walls and keeping them standing requires real effort.

Borders don't build themselves, and they don't stay strong without sustained effort. Despite the extra work, though, something deep within in us appreciates walls—or, at least, the idea of them. Walls imply safety and privacy and boundaries. Which is all fine—at least, to an extent. I'm glad my bathroom has walls, a ceiling, and a door that closes, and I'm better off for having established healthy boundaries in relationships. The problem isn't

---

[3] *The Poetry of Robert Frost,* ed. Edward Connery Lathem (New York: Henry Holt and Company, 1969), 33-34.

so much that walls exist but that we have a tendency to erect them in places that are neither helpful nor necessary.

Some of us rely disproportionately on unnecessary walls. We build them high and tight, hoping to hide the embarrassing parts of our lives and block access to the messy corners we'd prefer to keep hidden away. We invest our energies in keeping our walls high, thick, and impenetrable. We think as long as no one sees everything, all will be well. Except that's not how it works.

The problem with unnecessary walls is that the "protection" they offer quickly proves false. Instead of keeping us safe, needless walls isolate us in stuffy, separate squares, trapped with our own individual messes and ill-equipped to air grievances, shine light on injustice, or tackle big problems as a community.

The fallout?

- 70% of parents say they struggle to communicate meaningfully with their kids.[4]
- 57% of divorced couples cite communication problems as a contributing factor for their divorce.[5]
- 70% of employees are currently avoiding difficult conversations with their bosses, colleagues, or direct

---

[4] Robinson, Raz. "More Than Half of Parents Admit They Struggle to Hold a Conversation with Their Kids." *Fatherly.* *https://www.fatherly.com/news/survey-half-parents-struggle-hold-conversation-with-kids/* (Accessed November 29, 2019).

[5] Shaw, Gabbi. "These are the 11 most common reasons people get divorced, ranked." *Insider.* https://www.insider.com/why-people-get-divorced-2019-1 (Accessed December 30, 2019).

reports.[6]

- 53% of employees handle toxic situations by ignoring them.[7]
- 53% of Americans say talking about politics with people they disagree with is generally stressful and frustrating.[8]

It's hard to argue with statistics like those. They clearly demonstrate that, if possible, most people will avoid awkward conversations when they can. Worse, this tendency is only serving to drive us further apart.

It doesn't have to be this way.

What if there were a way to come together, like the neighbors in Frost's poem? We can keep our boundaries in place but set them at a level that will allow us to see one another, talk over the wall, and come together even as we find ourselves on different sides of the divide.

For that to happen, we'll need to open ourselves to the

---

[6] *Understanding the Conversation,* Braverly
https://learn.workbravely.com/hubfs/Understanding-the-Conversation-Gap.pdf?t=1533596048056&utm_campaign=smart%20brief%20test&utm_so urce=hs_automation&utm_medium=email&utm_content=64321921&_hsenc=p2ANqtz-_4k_KzRnQlCrerxB5Gr0XEMMWshlLmigMT3ElhTx6htsOUK3kcp7H-J_GAqZMvIAdILhbkkDX2sEDVSXIQdx9e-xqh8A&_hsmi=64321921 (Accessed November 29, 2019).

[7] Ibid.

[8] Pew Research Center. "More Now Say It's 'Stressful' to Discuss Politics With People They Disagree With." https://www.people-press.org/2018/11/05/more-now-say-its-stressful-to-discuss-politics-with-people-they-disagree-with/ (Accessed November 29, 2019).

likelihood of some fairly awkward conversations. Awkward conversations aren't necessarily bad. In fact, they can serve a very good purpose. The first step is to acknowledge that we need them—as individuals, societies, and Christian communities. We cannot function well without them.

Whom This Affects

Questioning is part of the human experience, and with the rise of internet use, many of our questions are now going directly to search engines. While we've all been known to search online for the occasional fact (say, what year World War II ended), in recent years, people have shifted from searching for confirmatory facts to searching the web for solutions. People are turning to the web for answers to their problems, and not just simple ones like "How do I get rid of bed bugs?" and "How do I get over jet lag?" They're turning to Google for help facing deep, meaningful issues, from "Why did I get married?" to "How to have sex?" and "What is the meaning of life?"[9] Of course, they're not asking Google. They're using Google as a tool to find articles, videos, and solutions from "experts"—which, on the internet, is definitely something you need to question. Because while Google's algorithm will ensure that searchers find the most popular answer, there's no guarantee they'll find one that's both truthful and compassionate.

---

[9] "The Most Asked Questions on Google." *Mondovo.*
https://www.mondovo.com/keywords/most-asked-questions-on-google (accessed December 7, 2019).

But why are people making these searches at all? Why are they turning to the internet as a first, last, or perhaps only resort? Why aren't they reaching out to friends, family members, faith leaders, and support systems instead?

Most people tend to avoid awkwardness when they can. Many would much rather type "Why do I have this weird rash?" into a search engine than consider showing their inflamed skin to another living, breathing human being. And when it comes to asking tough questions, they'd rather ask a search engine than a friend.

Believe me, I get it. I've had my share of rashes in my time, along with my share of questions I'm embarrassed to ask. I'm not one to shy away from confrontation, but even I'm guilty of avoiding awkward conversations from time to time.

In fact, on the day I outlined this very chapter, I found myself lingering in the frozen food section of my neighborhood market, intensely reading the packaging of some frozen potatoes. Not because I'm especially interested in the potassium and sodium levels but because I thought I'd seen someone out of the corner of my eye whom I just didn't have the bandwidth to engage. At least, that's what I told myself at the time. The truth was a little more complicated, and I wouldn't have confronted it directly if I hadn't been working on this chapter.

Why did I stand in the open door of the freezer aisle, living a lie and shivering as I pretended to ponder potatoes? Because this person and I have a history. At one time, we'd been friends, but our relational breakdown hadn't been within my control. This person had abruptly departed from our church under strained circumstances. I wasn't exactly part of the situation that had led to the departure, but I had grown up in church. Spending my entire life either with family members in church leadership or being a leader myself, I'd been on the receiving end of more than my share of misplaced hostility. I'd never quite learned to navigate these situations with grace. As a result of that long history—more so than my history with the person in question on that day—I felt I didn't have the energy to deal with whatever was about to happen when our eyes met. At least, that's what I told myself. So, I stood in the notch of an open freezer door, praying for the glass to fog over quickly and shield me.

Who Will Stand in the Gap?

In Ezekiel 22, God sends his prophet to confront the inhabitants of Jerusalem for their sins. He lists them in detail. They've shed blood, slandered others, worshiped idols, and committed lewd sexual acts. Their leaders—the princes, priests, and prophets—have been systematically abusing their power, profaning God's holiness while covering for each other's indiscretions. Extortion, oppression, and injustice reigned. In the midst of this, God says he's looked for a mediator, someone to stand in the gap as Moses had done during the wilderness wanderings. "But," God says, "I found none."[10]

This isn't to say that God can't find things when he looks for them or that he can't raise up righteous people when they're needed. In making this statement audible, he is proving a point—

---

[10] Ezekiel 22:30.

21

much like a mom who's asked her daughter countless times to put on her shoes and eventually peeks into her child's room, saying, "I'm looking for a little girl with shoes on so I can take her to the park, but I can't find one." The point isn't God's lack but ours. Left to ourselves, we don't naturally rise up, confront oppressors, rebuke sin and wickedness, deal with tough issues, ask awkward questions. It's in our nature to seek an easy way out.

Without God's direct intervention, we would be done for. Humanity is lost, and we cannot save ourselves. Fortunately, there is One who came to serve as ultimate Mediator between sinners and a holy God. In response to our lack of ability, Jesus came incarnate, walked among us, and endured the shame of the Cross. But it was impossible for death to hold him. Jesus is now risen from the dead, ascended, and sitting at the right hand of God the Father, ever interceding on our behalf.

Thank God for Jesus!

As disciples of the One who calls Himself the Way, the Truth, and the Life, we are called to follow his steps. One way we do so is by fulfilling the role of mediator. Just as the moon only reflects the light of the sun, so we only reflect a portion of Jesus' work as the true Mediator. Though we don't mediate directly between God and humankind in the same way Jesus does, we are tasked with becoming what Paul calls ministers of reconciliation.

> Therefore, if anyone is in Christ, he is a new creation. The old has passed away; behold, the new has come. All this is from God, who through Christ reconciled us to himself and gave us the ministry of

reconciliation; that is, in Christ God was reconciling the world to himself, not counting their trespasses against them, and entrusting to us the message of reconciliation. Therefore, we are ambassadors for Christ, God making his appeal through us. We implore you on behalf of Christ, be reconciled to God. For our sake he made him to be sin who knew no sin, so that in him we might become the righteousness of God.[11]

Jesus did the work that allowed us to be reconciled to God—a work that involved suffering, pain, shame, and death. As ones who have received the benefits of his labors, we're in a better position (and should be all the more motivated) to become reconcilers ourselves. That means we not only point others toward reconciliation in Christ, but we also show the world what it looks like to be reconciled with God and with each other. This doesn't happen on its own. It is an active work. Because we have been justified, we now do justice. Because we're at peace with God, we now seek peace and pursue it.[12]

In answering such a call, we cannot reasonably expect to avoid discomfort. No task involving such demanding verbs could ever be easy. Nor can we act as reconcilers if we're intent on building unnecessary walls to keep others out and our own messes safely hidden. No more hiding behind fogged glass clutching our bags of frozen potatoes.

---

[11] II Corinthians 5:17-21.
[12] Micah 6:8; 1 Peter 3:11.

If we're to take our spiritual responsibilities seriously, we must be willing to do the right thing when it's necessary. To be brave, step out in faith, overcome our awkwardness, and engage tough topics.

Start Your Own Awkward Conversation

Find some trusted conversation partners for discussion or consider the following questions on your own.

1. Describe one of your own Frozen Potatoes Moments, recalling a time when you knew you should have confronted a tough topic or situation but instead willfully avoided it.

2. Life requires boundaries. How can you tell which boundaries are healthy (that protect) or unhealthy (that trap/hide)? How can you tell the difference in your own life?

3. What might be involved in identifying and dismantling unnecessary walls?

4. What tough topics are you prone to avoiding and why?

5. How is your Christian responsibility as a reconciler involved in tackling tough topics?

Welcome to Awkwardsville:
Private Showing

Recently, I attended a movie by myself. This is something I hardly ever do, but I'd spent the entire day clamped to the keyboard and wanted an activity that would take me out of the house and then shut down my brain completely. I hadn't been able to rustle up someone to meet me at the theatre on such short notice, so there I was. Alone.

This took place knee-deep in the holiday shopping season, and traffic along my planned route is notoriously snarly that time of year. To be on the safe side, I left the house with plenty of time to spare. For whatever reason, however, I sailed right through even the tricky intersections, catching all green lights.

So not only was I seeing a movie by myself, but I was also early. Not that this is a rare situation for me—I have a tendency toward promptness. It usually means I arrive two or three minutes before the scheduled time.

But that wasn't the case this time. I pulled into the parking lot and glanced at my dashboard clock. This wasn't a few minutes early. This was awkwardly early. Even factoring in a trip to the ladies' room and a wait to get snacks, I'd still have more time than I plausibly needed. The theatre doors probably weren't even open yet. Rather than stand in the hall clutching my nachos and waiting for the staff to sweep the aisles from the last showing, I decided to read in my car.

I rolled my Ford Focus into an empty section of the lot, parked under the doubtful shade of a palm tree, and cracked the windows. Yes, it was December, but we're talking December in Florida. Satisfied I wouldn't suffocate during the wait, I flipped open my library app, content to sneak in a quick chapter or two while waiting.

That's when it happened. An SUV pulled into the space directly facing mine.

The motion of the vehicle caught my attention, and I glanced up just in time to see the driver shift into park, shut off the engine, lean over, and plant a huge, juicy kiss on the woman in the passenger's seat. She responded enthusiastically, and within seconds, they transitioned into a full make-out session.

I'd parked out behind the theatre, at the back of the lot. Every other space in that section was completely empty. The fact that they'd parked directly in front of me was odd.

What was even worse was how long this kiss was lasting. I peeked, just to check. Yes, this was a long kiss. So, so long.

There I sat in my little car, quietly sweating—now for multiple reasons—peering through my windshield at this impromptu exhibition. My brain followed several lines of thought at the same time.

Wow, they are really going at it.

Did they realize I was here when they parked?

If so, did they care that I was watching?

Wait—was that why they'd parked here in the first place?

So that I would watch?

How dare they.

Wait, why was I still watching?

I dropped my eyes to the steering wheel. At some point, I'd also dropped my phone and was now grasping the wheel as if to drive away, which I seriously wanted to do. But if I started the car, they'd hear me and realize I'd been watching, and whether this was what they wanted or not, it was a situation so awkward I couldn't even contemplate it.

Leaning down to scramble for my phone and keys, I snatched them up, slipped from the car (closing the door very gently), and scuttled into the theatre. I halted as I neared the door. Why was I running? I was still way early. *Slow down.*

My internal orders didn't work. All too soon, I was standing outside the doors to Auditorium 10, waiting for two teenagers to clear the room from the previous show, awkwardly clutching my plastic tray of nachos, and yearning to explain to anyone walking by and willing to make eye contact that, honestly, I didn't mean to be this early.

Socially Awkward

CHAPTER 2
Willing to Go There

I was going to make a difference. I just knew it. Back in the year 2000, I was a bright-eyed first-year teacher, setting up her classroom and eagerly anticipating an endless succession of "Oh Captain, My Captain!" moments like in *Dead Poet's Society*. The only thing that scared me was the fear that one of my students might ask a question I wouldn't know how to answer. Just the thought of saying "I don't know" made me writhe.

Oh, young Ruth. How I wish I could let you in on three little secrets.

1) It will happen constantly.

2) The more often it happens, the less it will bother you.

3) Being repeatedly forced to admit your ignorance in front of a group who shows no mercy will prove one of the most formative experiences of your life.

The lessons forged in the fires of my first-year classroom are still playing out in my daily life. I mean, I still don't like saying "I don't know," but the words slip out more easily with practice. I'm ashamed to think how hard I resisted saying them for so long.

Maybe that's my personality. Maybe it's the foolish pride of youth. Maybe it's a toxic combination of the two. But for a long time, admitting ignorance was something I avoided at all costs.

The joke, however, was wholly on me. Avoiding the words didn't keep them from being true—or hide that truth from anyone but me. There was, in fact, much I didn't know—and still don't.

Off the Hook

When it comes to having awkward conversations, sometimes what holds us back isn't so much fear of speaking up but fear of not knowing exactly what to say. We haven't completely researched the subject. We don't have first-hand experience. We're aware there's need for nuance. And we're not sure how best to communicate that.

I want to let you off the hook right away. You don't have to know everything in order to say something. This book explores a lot of sensitive issues, but it doesn't serve as the be-all, end-all authority on any of them. Pressing into awkward conversations is less about having all the right answers and more about discovering how to discuss tough topics effectively.

As we progress, we'll examine the instincts that prompt us to avoid potentially awkward topics and learn how to flip the script and engage in compelling, meaningful conversations while lessening the chances we'll damage relationships in the process.

What's the Point?

Recently, I engaged in an honest conversation with a young child about the stress of playing board games. She's always excited as we're setting up the board—but then the game begins, and it all starts going south. She wishes she could enjoy family game night more, but once things get going, she's so stressed that she can't truly enjoy herself. Her mood swings are wildly disproportionate: giddy elation if she wins and total devastation if she loses. Real, boiling tears—shuddery sobs. It's painful to watch.

After affirming her feelings (I mean honestly, who actually likes losing?), I told her she might enjoy games more if she put them in their proper place. Part of growing up is realizing that the point of playing a game isn't necessarily the game itself—the point is to have fun with family and friends. If she can see board games as a fun way to bond with the people she loves—make connecting with them her goal instead of winning the game—she might learn to enjoy that aspect even when she loses.

Meaningful communication isn't a game, and we shouldn't treat it lightly; however, when it comes to having awkward conversations about hard topics, it would be helpful if we approached such moments with a similar board-game mentality. We must not assume that the only way we'll get something out of the conversation is if we "win" (that is, prove our perspective is right and the other person is wrong). We must remember that what matters most in a conversation isn't the point we're trying to make but the person we're making it to.

Tackling tough conversations isn't about proving ourselves

right but about helping our communities flourish. When engaging in uncomfortable conversations, "winning" is a cheap substitute for our real objective. Remember, we are ministers of reconciliation. In pressing through discomfort and engaging in tough topics, our motivation must always be love of God and love of neighbor.

What Holds Us Back

Often, we hold back from awkward conversations due to the very natural fear that we'll be asked questions we can't answer or be required to provide solutions for seemingly insurmountable problems.

Remember, awkward conversations aren't always about answers. Often, they're about acknowledging pain, standing in solidarity next to our friends, and staring complex issues in the face without retreating in fear. Often, they're less about solving problems and more about sympathizing, empathizing, and commiserating with people facing harsh realities in a world beset with sin, pain, and death. Sometimes all we can do is share our hurt, confusion, and inadequacy with one another as we gaze together at an issue from different angles, reminded that only God is all-knowing and all-sufficient. Through these conversations, answers come.

Sometimes we help and build bridges to hope.

Sometimes not.

Sometimes we just show up.

That's okay.

Awkward conversations are hard work, and we shouldn't pretend otherwise.

Follow His Steps

Let's not sugarcoat it. None of this is easy. But we must press into the tough topics, if for no other reason than we are called to follow the footsteps of our Savior Jesus Christ, who had awkward conversations all the time. Seriously.

If you don't believe me, sit down with a pencil, a little notepad, and read the Gospels. If you don't have time to read them all, any single Gospel will do, but for this exercise, Luke and John are my personal favorites. Start reading, and as you go, make a little check mark every time Jesus says something that contradicts, challenges, opposes, or downright baffles people. My absolute favorite moments are when Jesus says things that manage to upset everyone at the same time—critics and followers alike. When you come across one of those instances, add a bonus mark.

One of the clearest examples—and my personal favorite—is recorded in John 6. Shortly after Jesus multiplied the bread and fish to feed the multitudes, the crowds tracked him down with a request. They wanted to see another sign. In trying to talk him into doing their bidding, the Jews cagily remind Jesus that their ancestors had eaten manna in the wilderness. The subtext here is that if Jesus were really divine, he'd do something similar for them. Then they'd really believe. But Jesus wasn't having it. Their fathers ate manna in the wilderness and still died, he reminded them. So, what was the benefit in that? He hadn't come just to give them unlimited fresh bread but to give them himself. Only, he didn't say it quite like that.

> "I am the living bread that came down from heaven. If anyone eats of this bread, he will live forever. And the bread that I will give for the life of the world is my flesh."
>
> The Jews then disputed among themselves, saying, "How can this man give us his flesh to eat?"
>
> So Jesus said to them, "Truly, truly, I say to you, unless you eat the flesh of the Son of Man and drink his blood, you have no life in you. Whoever feeds on my flesh and drinks my blood has eternal life, and I will raise him up on the last day. For my flesh is true food, and my blood is true drink. Whoever feeds on my flesh and drinks my blood abides in me, and I in him. As the living Father sent me, and I live because of the Father, so whoever feeds on me, he also will live because of me. This is the bread that came down from heaven, not like the bread the fathers ate, and died. Whoever feeds on this bread will live forever."[13]

Imagine being in the crowd for that moment. I wish I had been there, if just to see eyes widen, stances shift, to hear the sounds of shock and disgust the crowds no doubt would have made.

---

[13] John 6:49-58.

In retrospect, of course, we understand Jesus' point. He didn't come just to give good gifts: he himself is the gift. But think about how the conversation actually went down. They ask for bread, and he tells them they'll drink his blood and eat his flesh. Talk about awkward.

His own disciples barely knew how to handle it. "This is a hard saying," they inform him. An understatement if ever there was one.

And this awkward conversation? From a human perspective, it doesn't go so well. John 6 closes with the news that "After this many of his disciples turned back and no longer walked with him," and Chapter 7 opens by stating that the Jews are now actively seeking to kill Jesus.[14]

This isn't the only place Scripture records Jesus upsetting nearly everybody at the same time. It's worth noting as well that John says the written record of this period does not contain everything Jesus said and did.[15] We can only speculate about the number of hard sayings Jesus incorporated in his interactions, what ratio they took up in his communication, and how often both friends and foes walked away scratching their heads.

One thing we know for sure is that while vast multitudes followed Jesus for a time, not many stuck around over the long haul. By the time we get to the opening of the book of Acts and read what takes place among his followers after the crucifixion, Luke records that only one hundred and twenty believers have gathered to decide who would replace Judas. Even more to the

---

[14] John 6:66; 7:1.
[15] John 21:25.

point, when Peter proposes choosing "from among the men who have accompanied us during the whole time the Lord Jesus went in and out among us," only two people fit the bill.[16] That means other than the twelve whom Jesus called out specifically by name, only two other men had stayed the course and followed Jesus from start to finish.[17]

With all the evidence before us, we can't claim Jesus avoided tough conversations and only told people what they wanted to hear. In fact, he often went out of his way to do the opposite. If we're commanded to follow Jesus' steps, what does that mean for us? And what might it look like in our daily lives if we attempted to follow his lead?

Good Friction

The word *friction* has developed a bad reputation, largely undeserved. Think about the way we use this word. We use it to describe difficult relationships. ("There's some friction between us.") We blame it for blisters and chafing. But it's important to note that while chafing can certainly bring about bad or destructive effects, it can also bring about positive ones. Chafing may cause discomfort when it creates abrasions on the skin, but it keeps your hands warm when temperatures drop. The same sort of friction that can start forest fires also sparks cheery campfires over which you can cook dinner or toast marshmallows.

---

[16] Acts 1:15-23.

[17] Scriptural evidence is less clear about the size of the group of women who followed Jesus and served him faithfully through his earthly ministry.

Whether you view friction as damaging or as helpful is all about context—how friction's applied, when, why, and what boundaries are set to keep it under control. While bad friction hurts and destroys, good friction keeps us safe, warm, and stable. Friction allows us to walk where we want and choose at what speed we get there. It allows us to pick up and hold objects and hug each other.

On the other hand, bad friction puts us in danger, harms us, and can potentially kill us. The fact that friction contains such inherent dangers, however, shouldn't cause us to seek a purely frictionless life. While bad friction should rightly be avoided when possible, good friction is absolutely necessary for life and human flourishing.

We couldn't live in a physically frictionless world, and we can't truly flourish in a figuratively frictionless one, either. Our social, emotional, and spiritual lives depend on the traction provided by good friction.

What Is Good Friction?

Good friction often results as we come together from differing backgrounds, beliefs, cultures, and philosophies, allowing our deepest underlying assumptions about the world, our place in it, and how everything fits together to come in direct contact. Good friction arises during these encounters when we seek new information, ask clarifying questions, provide alternate perspectives, and speak truth even when it might prove relationally costly. At one time or another, we should find ourselves either on the giving or receiving end of such friction. Good friction is the "iron sharpening iron" mentioned in Proverbs 27:17, describing how we shape each other's lives through the natural friction that results from living in close community.

If we're going to cultivate relationships with any sort of depth, the question isn't whether we're going to encounter friction. The question is how we handle it when it comes.

How Do We Handle Friction?

When it comes to handling friction, most people fall into three major categories: those who allow it, those who abuse it, and those who avoid it.

Allowing Friction

Allowing friction doesn't mean we always enjoy it or even approve of it in all circumstances. It just means we're not averse to coexisting with friction for a season. We're willing to let difficult conversations and awkward situations play out, opening ourselves to the possibility that good friction can bring positive results. Allowing friction means you don't avoid awkward situations, people, or conversations. You let them unfold. In other words, no hiding in the frozen food aisle.

That doesn't mean you necessarily take your hands off or let the friction catch fire and rage out of control. It simply means you recognize the necessary role friction plays in emotional maturity and spiritual formation. Because you acknowledge the potential harm that could result if allowed to continue unchecked, you put healthy parameters in place to ensure that friction is properly used for helpful purposes.

Think about sandpaper. It's rough and scratchy, but if we want smooth corners on our wooden furniture, judicious use of sandpaper is required. During the process of sanding these edges down, we may have to endure an uncomfortable period of noise, scratching, and wood dust flying everywhere; however, we're willing to endure temporary discomfort for the sake of the finished product.

In the same way, if we're going to let good friction do its work in our relationships, we may go through temporary periods of discomfort, annoyance, and yes—sometimes even pain. But if the end result is positive change, it's worth counting the cost, investing the time and energy, and working toward a better outcome.

Avoiding Friction

The reasons people shut down friction are many, running the gamut from self-preserving to downright nefarious.

- People who have been hurt or abused in the past can sometimes be especially sensitive to even the slightest discomfort in relationships. While this makes some more adept at navigating friction, it makes others back away more quickly in order to protect themselves and/or the relationship.
- People who hold power may be interested in maintaining control and therefore view any friction as a threat to their tightly managed status quo. When different perspectives

are raised or new viewpoints discussed, they may shut down any hint of debate, admonishing others to "Be a team player" and "Know your place." They quell even legitimate questions, comments, and concerns about their methods and practices, all in the guise of getting along.

Of course, these are two extremes. We shouldn't overlook the fact that specific circumstances influence this dynamic as well. Everything from cultural norms, personality types, and individual histories can factor into how people deal with conflict.

Rather than taking the time to discuss in detail all the reasons why someone might avoid conflict, I'd rather focus on the harm this tendency can do. Those who consistently shut down any hint of friction immediately could be just as damaging as those who deploy it in harmful and abusive ways.

Take, for example, a younger brother who is being bullied by his older sister. If the two begin squabbling over an incident of bullying, it might be tempting for the parent who didn't observe the entire event to seek an immediate end to the strife by telling them simply to stop fighting—to rely on the old "I don't care who started it—I'm going to finish it." What the parent is seeking here is a temporary absence of friction. What the younger child is seeking, however, is justice—which a shutting down of friction without proper investigation would not bring. This example is mirrored both on the small and the grand scale, played out in homes, classrooms, board rooms, and national governments around the world.

A lifetime avoiding friction is antithetical to a lifetime of following the scriptural mandate to do justice, love mercy, and walk humbly with God.[18]

Abusing Friction

Just as there are arsonists who light fires on purpose, so there are people who purposefully stir up strife. This isn't a good thing. In Scripture, strife is specifically noted as a work of the flesh (Galatians 5:19-21) and is associated with false teachers (1 Timothy 6:3-5), fools (Proverbs 20:3), scoffers (Proverbs 22:10), transgressors (Proverbs 17:19-20), and troublemakers (Proverbs 16:28). Though strife can spring from many motivations, Scripture is clear about its roots in pride (Proverbs 13:9-10), evil desires (James 4:1), hatred (Proverbs 10:12), greed (Proverbs 28:25), and wrath (Proverbs 15:18).

When we recognize that someone is indeed stirring up strife for sinful of selfish motivations, how are we to handle it? We certainly aren't to respond in kind. Fighting fire with fire might occasionally be a smart tactic in the real world of firefighting, but it's certainly not a metaphorical tactic we can apply. It's not something we saw Jesus model, nor is it a behavior endorsed in Scripture.

When instructing younger pastor Timothy, Paul admonishes him: to "flee youthful passions and pursue righteousness, faith, love, and peace, along with those who call on the Lord from a pure heart. Have nothing to do with foolish, ignorant controversies; you know that they breed quarrels." Paul continues that the Lord's

---

[18] Micah 6:8.

servant "must not be quarrelsome but kind to everyone, able to teach, patiently enduring evil, correcting his opponents with gentleness. God may perhaps grant them repentance leading to a knowledge of the truth, and they may come to their senses and escape from the snare of the devil, after being captured by him to do his will."[19]

This is sound advice, and not just for those in pastoral ministry. It's an approach that all generations need to hear repeated and see modeled by their elders.

Not all friction is good. As indicated in the previous sections, in order for friction to be classified "good," it must be kept under control and used as a temporary measure intended for the purposes of refinement. Practicing discernment in this area won't be easy, but being aware of the dynamic will, at the very least, keep you from taking an all-or-nothing approach to dealing with friction.

A Different Attitude

Stupid arguments lead to quarrels. Spend more than a few minutes scrolling through any social media platform, listening to conversations in waiting rooms, or enduring talking-head segments on cable news channels, and you will see enough evidence to last a lifetime. As Paul reminded Timothy, this is not the way of the Christian. Rather than allowing the fools who are stirring up strife to draw us into their foolishness, we are to meet their friction with a completely different attitude.

---

[19] 2 Timothy 2:22-26.

Timothy is admonished to be kind, patient, forgiving, and gentle even when he is instructing those who hold foolish opinions. This is not so that he can feel righteous and lord it over them, but so that those who have gone astray may have the opportunity to repent and change. Timothy may find it easier to adopt this attitude if he remembers that these people are being blinded and held captive by the devil and need to be freed by the truth.[20]

As Jesus showed us in his interactions both with the religious elite and his everyday followers, the goal in correcting fools is not simply to show them how wrong they are. It's to light the pathway by which they and others observing can potentially see truth. Our goal should not be to defeat people. It should be to warn and welcome them. When it comes to dealing with "foolish and ignorant controversies," some of us may need to consider how Scriptural admonitions line up with our current approach. Ask the Spirit for wisdom to discern the vital from the trivial. Then, if necessary, recalibrate.[21]

In approaching awkward conversations, the goal is neither to live an entirely frictionless life nor to fan flames unnecessarily. The goal is to leverage "good friction" for the common good.

---

[20] Paul Premsekaran Cornelius, "2 Timothy" in *South Asia Bible Commentary*, ed. Brian Wintle (Grand Rapids: Zondervan, 2015), 1696.

[21] An early iteration of the ideas in this section first appeared on my Twitter timeline on February 5, 2021. https://twitter.com/RuthMBuchanan/status/1357771925926400003 (Accessed February 5, 2021).

Practically Speaking

These issues are much easier to talk about in theory than to break down realistically and put into practice. You still may not be sure what it all might entail. That's all right. We will get there.

For now, as you consider the role of good friction and its place in difficult conversations, you'll likely recognize that you have a tendency to lean too far one way or the other. Either you're prone to taking combative stances by playing the devil's advocate, or you tend to back away from confrontation, avoiding friction even when it's clearly needed. Whichever course correction you require, I pray that you find it. Your ability to engage others effectively on tough topics depends on it.

Start Your Own Awkward Conversation

Find some trusted conversation partners for discussion or consider the questions on your own.

1. Do you tend to shut down friction or engage with it? Has this tendency proven helpful or harmful in your life? Why? Give some examples.

2. In your opinion, what might constitute good friction? What parameters should be placed on moments of friction to keep them from blazing out of control and causing harm?

3. How can you recognize good friction and differentiate it from the bad? How would you handle someone who chooses to employ friction in a way that's clearly abusive or harmful?

4. What instance depicted in Scripture caused many of Jesus's followers to walk away during his earthly ministry? What spiritual lessons about our relationship with him and others can we draw from this?

5. What could we gain by pressing through discomfort to engage socially awkward conversations despite the potential for friction?

Welcome to Awkwardsville:
The Time I Stopped Soccer Practice

I've never been a soccer mom. I have, however, been a soccer aunt. A few years ago, it was my turn for Friday night soccer duty with my two young nephews. I drove them across town to the sprawl of fields surrounding the soccer club where I lugged my beach chair and a book out to the sidelines. I settled in for a comfortable evening of swatting mosquitoes.

Truth be told, I did less reading than I planned and a lot more laughing. If you've ever watched junior youth league soccer, you know why.

- At one point, a little boy attempted what may have been a poorly executed bicycle kick. He missed the ball entirely, hollering, "SON of a *NUT*!" Meanwhile, behind him, my younger nephew turned a crooked line of solo cartwheels, completely detached from the drama unfolding around him.
- A boy on the next field yelled, "Coach, when are we gonna play sharps and minnows?" I know he said *sharps*

instead of *sharks* because he yelled this on a loop for forty-five minutes.

- Around sunset, a bird pooped while flying over the field. It was very exciting. "I saw the poop come out. It looked like a bunch of little strings. It almost landed on your head, Carlos!"

On it went. If I were, in fact, a soccer mom who routinely sat on the sidelines, I may have been bored by all this. As a mere soccer aunt who just stepped in from time to time, I was finding everything hilarious.

Well, not everything. I'd brought two boys, and their practices did not run concurrently, unfortunately. After an hour and a half, we switched fields for practice number two. I let the boys run together to the next field while I gathered up my chair, keys, phone, and book before following.

When I arrived at the second practice field, however, I couldn't spot my younger nephew. Meanwhile, my older nephew's practice didn't seem to have started. He stood among a disorganized cluster of sweaty little boys, goofing around and kicking the ball willy-nilly.

I caught his eye and motioned for him to leave the group and come over. Instead of immediate compliance, he merely shot me an uncomfortable look and continued kicking the ball with his friends.

I called his name.

He frowned, waved, and shook his head. He continued playing. The nerve! Such a direct rejection of my authority was not to be borne.

I dropped my chair and book on the sidelines and stalked into the middle of the cluster. One of the older boys, ignoring my presence, kicked the ball toward my nephew. I extended a foot and stopped the ball, trapping it under the sole of my sneaker. I'm not very sporty—or very coordinated at all—and was secretly proud of myself. No one else seemed impressed. But never mind. I wasn't here for glory.

I pinned my nephew to the turf with my eyes. "Where is your brother?"

He swiped his forearms across his face to clear the sweat. "In the bathroom."

"And why didn't you answer when I called you?"

He blinked. "Because we're practicing." He gestured toward the older boy, who was staring at me as if I had sprouted horns. I came to the slow realization that he wasn't just a little bit older than the other boys. He was a lot older.

In fact, he was their coach. He was a coach, they'd already started practicing, and I'd just stalked onto the field and stomped the ball in the middle of a drill.

The best way to weather the shame was to pretend I didn't feel it.

"Well. Okay. Good. Fine. Alrighty, then. Have a good time, folks." I lifted my foot from the ball and gave it a tap before backing slowly off the field, praying a sinkhole would open behind me.

Socially Awkward

CHAPTER 3
Anything but Black and White

I'm carrying on a lifelong love affair with books. The more I read, the more often I am completely blown away by all the things I don't know—indeed, by how much I'm not even aware that I don't know. It's extremely humbling, but apparently this is how love affairs go. Every long-term relationship comes with a cost, and in the case of mine with books, the cost has been my pride.

A commitment to lifelong learning is a commitment to humility and the daily willingness to own areas in which we've been wrong or uninformed up to this point.[22] This is especially true of the Christian, for whom a lifetime of learning coincides with a lifetime of submission to the Holy Spirit. Everything we glean from books is filtered by the Spirit through what we know via both general and special revelation. Once the wheel of wisdom gets cranking, the results are truly dramatic.

Over the past few years, I've purposefully and vigorously

---

[22] Ruth Buchanan. "I Have the Spiritual Gift of Reading." *Fathom Magazine.* https://www.fathommag.com/stories/i-have-the-spiritual-gift-of-reading (Accessed December 30, 2019).

expanded my interaction with history. I'm not talking about reading historical novels or history textbooks, which both have their fine points and weaknesses. I'm talking instead about intentionally reading books written about (but especially during) specific eras. As I've been able, I've traveled to some of the locations I've read about, walking the grounds myself, meeting people, conducting interviews, listening and learning from those who were there when it happened.[23] I've begun to learn how much I missed in school while simultaneously realizing the deep spiritual implications of this knowledge. Along the way, I've learned that America's track record is more checkered than I'd been led to believe from the super patriotic curriculum my schools had favored in the 1980s-90s. Especially as it relates to issues surrounding race and racism in America. They're anything but black and white.

Looking Back

The more I've read, the more I've become convinced that many Americans have trouble talking about racial issues at least in part because we don't carry a shared vision of our country's history. This is a problem. The threads of the past run through the fabric of the present, and the extent to which we grasp that reality affects both our perspective on the present and potential resolutions for the future.

---

[23] At the time of this writing, the ongoing coronavirus pandemic has temporarily halted this aspect of my re-education.

Because we lack a shared vision of history, however, we're forever misunderstanding one another. Personally, I'm always walking the tension between letting what I feel to be misinformed comments slide and developing a reputation as the "Well Actually" Girl.

The "Well Actually" Girl is the version of me who dons a parachute and drops into conversations uninvited, megaphone clutched in hand, ready to trumpet her historical perspectives directly into the faces of anyone unfortunate enough to be standing within range. Each fresh monologue starts with this dreaded phrase, "Well, *actually . . .* "

I'm honestly trying not to be that person. Nobody likes the "Well Actually" Girl, and I can't say I'm too fond of her, either. I'm trying to spare us all from this. But circumstances aren't making it easy. The more I learn about the unvarnished past, the more I find my perspectives diverging from those of my peers.

Today, I'll share just one of these perspective shifts with you. We'll then discuss why such perspectives are helpful in framing discussions surrounding race and racism in America, and why we should keep talking about things like this, even when it's awkward. Perhaps especially when it is awkward.

Perspective: The Asian-American Experience

A few years ago, some friends and I planned to get together for a hot pot dinner. Because we were meeting at my house, I agreed to supply the hot pot and the soup base. At the nearby Chinese grocery store, I accidentally chose a mega-spicy

Szechwan soup base. I wish I could claim this was a rookie mistake, but honestly, it was just carelessness. While I was there, I grabbed a few snacks for my nieces and nephews to try. The snacks were a hit, and through the rest of that summer, we started visiting the store frequently together to try new treats.

Initially, the kids couldn't tell the difference between Chinese, Korean, Japanese, or Thai products, nor could they recognize a difference in the languages spoken by other customers. That didn't surprise me. What did surprise me was that certain ones wouldn't take my word for it that the proprietor was Chinese.

"How do you know?"

"Well, he speaks Chinese."

"Speaking Chinese doesn't make you Chinese."

Which was a fair point. But the proprietor is Chinese. The kids who were with me just didn't have the cultural savvy to recognize this. This isn't to tear them down. They simply lacked experience and context. I was the same way at their age.

I grew up largely undereducated about Asia—the most populous (and arguably the most vibrant and diverse) continent in the world. I tended to lump the entire region and its diverse groups all together in my mind—Asians from Asia. Then, as an adult, I spent some time in that part of the globe. Which isn't to say I know everything—or even very much. Probably the best thing that happened to me was realizing not just how much I didn't know but also how much I didn't *know* I didn't know. This experience led to changed perspectives. This new perspective influenced more than just my understanding of the world. It changed my understanding of others—but also of myself.

Immigration

My maternal grandfather immigrated to the United States when he was just a boy. My mother and her brother were first-generation Americans on that side of the family, and therefore my siblings and I could technically be considered second-generation Americans. Only we never thought of ourselves in those terms. That's because our grandfather immigrated from Sweden. He was tall, with a barrel chest, blond hair, and blue eyes. His name was changed at Ellis Island, shortened and abbreviated to something that was intended to sound more distinctly American than Scandinavian. Once he learned English and lost his accent, he could completely blend into his surroundings. By the time my siblings and I came along, there was no talk of us being from a Scandinavian-American family. Personally, for a long time, I didn't think much about my generational ethnic identity. I just thought of myself as your garden-variety American. But that's a privilege everyone doesn't enjoy equally, I've since discovered.

While a second-generation European immigrant kid like me can easily and fully blend into the broader American culture, Asian-Americans attest to a different experience. Even born and raised in this country, they still tend to be seen as outsiders.

Because many cross-sections of our fellow Americans know so little about Asian countries, they tend to be underequipped to ask even basic questions about ethnicity and family origin. Asian-Americans report that they're often asked where they're from; but when they say they're from Philly or Fort Lauderdale, they're then asked, "No, where are you *really* from?" As if it's impossible for someone of Asian descent to *really* be from Philly. This interaction is so pervasive that sociologists have given it a nickname: The Perpetual Foreigner Syndrome.

Though Asians currently seem to occupy a positive place in America's racial structure, viewed largely as a "model minority" due to their perceived work ethic and socioeconomic achievements, they're still viewed as perpetual foreigners because of their physical characteristics.[24] When these identifications are considered side-by-side, being both Model Minority and Perpetual Foreigner, the result is a complicated social reality—one that differs significantly from my own.

Given what people of Asian descent encounter, I'm not surprised when they voice a different experience in America than those who, like me, are of European descent. Especially considering further complications due to the historical realities faced by past Asian immigrants in America.

In considering the history of my own people on these shores, I know of no laws and legislation passed to actively work against the settlement of the Swedish-American population in the United States. Discrimination against Swedes has never really been a thing. The same cannot be said for Asian minority groups, particularly Chinese and Japanese.

Chinese Exclusion Act

In the latter half of the nineteenth century, the discovery of gold in the Western American states coincided with a period of

---

[24] Min Zhou, "Asians in America: The Paradox of 'The Model Minority' and 'The Perpetual Foreigner,'" abstract, University of Saskatchewan Sorokin Lecture (February 9, 2012).

civil unrest in southern China. Between 1850 and 1852, Chinese immigration to California and the Pacific Northwest jumped from several hundred a year to tens of thousands.[25] Chinese arrivals established vibrant and flourishing communities, brought goods and services, and—for a time—they thrived.

It was this very thriving, though, that ultimately brought trouble. Apparently, these specific immigrants putting down roots and succeeding was perceived by some as a threat. In the spring of 1882, President Chester A. Arthur signed the Congress-proposed Chinese Exclusion Act, limiting Chinese immigration only to proven non-laborers. This marked the first time in American history that the Federal government banned entry of an ethnic working group on the premise that it "endangered the good order of certain localities."[26] How exactly had Chinese immigrants endangered the good order of their communities? They'd created competition with existing systems. Despite the fact that this is precisely how a free-market economy is designed to work, the success of Chinese immigrants prompted a deep and hostile backlash, and a growing sense of nativism led to pressure on the Federal government to impose restrictive actions.[27]

---

[25] The U.S. National Archives and Records Administration. "Affidavit and Flyers from the Chinese Boycott Case." Archives.gov. https://www.archives.gov/education/lessons/chinese-boycott (accessed July 10, 2018).

[26] Our Documents. "Chinese Exclusion Act, 1882." OurDocuments.gov. https://www.ourdocuments.gov/doc.php?flash=false&doc=47 (Accessed June 10, 2018).

[27] National Archives. "Chinese Immigration and the Chinese in the United States." https://www.archives.gov/research/chinese-americans/guide (Accessed June 10, 2018).

In the wake of the Chinese Exclusion Act came more discriminatory legislation. Chinese people were not allowed to testify against whites in court; schools and lodging houses were segregated; Chinese laundry services were subject to different licensing fees than non-Chinese ones; people of Chinese descent were forbidden to intermarry with whites and were often banned from certain sections of cities.[28] Newspapers in major cities published articles and cartoons mocking the Chinese. This merely served to stoke the flames of hatred. The animosity grew so volatile that it often boiled over into violence, both on the small and grand scale. In Los Angeles, it led directly to the Chinese Massacre of 1871, the worst incident of mass lynching that we know of in American history.[29]

From my earliest memory, I'd been raised with the notion that America was a melting pot. That from its founding, it had served as a land of welcome and opportunity for all, and that anyone could come here, work hard, and become successful, just as my grandfather had done.

In the case of Chinese immigrants, however, it was because they worked hard and succeeded that they were targeted for clear discrimination and—in some cases—extreme hatred and acts of violence. The Chinese weren't the only Asian groups to experience deep injustice at the hands of the American government, however.

---

[28] The U.S. National Archives and Records Administration, Ibid.

[29] Kelly Wallace. "Forgotten Los Angeles History: The Chinese Massacre of 1871" *Los Angeles Public Library*. https://www.lapl.org/collections-resources/blogs/lapl/chinese-massacre-1871 (Accessed February 9, 2021).

Japanese Internment

On December 7, 1941, the American military base in Pearl Harbor, Hawaii, was attacked by the Imperial Japanese Army. The next day, President Roosevelt declared war on Japan, and within an hour of his date-that-will-live-in-infamy speech, Congress voted nearly unanimously to support the war. (The only no-voter was jeered with boos and hisses.)[30]

Lines at enlistment offices spilled into the streets. In one of those lines was my maternal grandfather. He'd joined the Navy as a teen and had been previously stationed in Pearl Harbor. The thought of his buddies under attack galvanized him to re-enlist. He wanted to protect his friends and family from enemies abroad. Not all Americans believed that the enemy resided exclusively across the Pacific, though. Anger, rage, and bitter resentment churned in the hearts of many—not just against the enemy over there but of a perceived threat over here.

Americans of Japanese descent immediately came under nearly universal suspicion—as did any people who were perceived to look Japanese. Things got so bad that Asian Americans who were not Japanese would fly the flag of their ancestral homeland or wear little buttons when in public in an effort to distinguish themselves from Japanese Americans and avoid foul treatment.[31]

---

[30] Craig Shirley and Scott Mauer, "The Attack on Pearl Harbor United Americans Like No Other Event in Our History." *The Washington Post.* https://www.washingtonpost.com/posteverything/wp/2016/12/07/the-attack-on-pearl-harbor-united-americans-like-no-other-event-in-our-history/?utm_term=.440a1d566651 (accessed July 12, 2018).
[31] Rare Historical Photos. "Chinese Americans labeling themselves to avoid being confused with the hated Japanese Americans, 1941." May 17, 2017,

Over the next few months, the bad faith moved from the realm of emotions to large-scale action. And I'm not just talking about vigilantes. I'm talking about the full force of the government.

In March of 1942, four months after Imperial Japan's attack on Pearl Harbor, upwards of 120,000 Americans of Japanese ancestry—the majority of whom had been born in the United States themselves and were full-fledged, natural-born citizens—were forced to submit to Executive Order 9066.[32] Passed on the authority of a report filled with known falsehoods (like the reports of sabotage which were later revealed to be the result of cattle damaging power lines), this order required anyone as little as one-sixteenth Japanese to vacate their homes and report to control stations.[33] Though we know now what was in store for them, at the time of the order, what would happen beyond that was left to their imagination.

By that point, though, the order may have felt inevitable. Backlash against Japanese and Japanese Americans had begun mere hours after the bombing.

The roundups began quietly within forty-eight hours after the Japanese attacked Pearl Harbor on December 7, 1941. The announced purpose was to protect the West Coast. Significantly, the incarceration program got underway despite a warning that

---

https://rarehistoricalphotos.com/chinese-americans-during-ww2-1941/ (Accessed February 9, 2021).

[32] I found conflicting numbers in several sources, most of them bouncing between 117,000 to 120,000.

[33] The History Channel. "Japanese Internment Camps." February 21, 2020. https://www.history.com/topics/world-war-ii/japanese-american-relocation (Accessed February 9, 2021).

these measures were unnecessary.

In January 1942, a naval intelligence officer in Los Angeles reported that Japanese Americans were being perceived as a threat almost entirely "because of the physical characteristics of the people." Fewer than 3% of them might be inclined toward sabotage or spying, he wrote, and the Navy and the FBI already knew who most of those individuals were. Still, the government ignored this warning and took the position summed up by John DeWitt, the Army general in command of the coast: "A Jap's a Jap. They are a dangerous element, whether loyal or not."[34]

Individuals and families were forced to leave their lives and livelihoods behind. Japanese American business owners were only given a short time to liquidate their possessions, often at great loss. Many had no recourse but to accept whatever lowball offers were given them, selling cars for $25 and entire hotels for $500.[35]

From 1942 to 1945, these Americans lived as refugees in their own land. Sent to camps across the West, Midwest, and South, they were incarcerated under armed guard. Though internees were allowed to stay with their families for the most part, they experienced a low quality of life inside the camps, including makeshift sanitation, poor nutrition, and harsh treatment from the

---

[34] T.A. Frail, "The Injustice of Japanese-American Internment Camps Resonates Strongly to This Day." Smithsonian.org. January 2017, https://www.smithsonianmag.com/history/injustice-japanese-americans-internment-camps-resonates-strongly-180961422/ (Accessed July 11, 2018).
[35] John Hersey, "A Mistake of Terrifically Horrible Proportions" in *Manzanar: Ansel Adam's Lost Photographic Document of a Tragic Secret in the American Past—the Japanese-American Internment Camp at Manzanar,* ed. John Armor and Peter Wright (New York: Vintage Books, 1988), 4-5.

guards.[36]

When the camps were finally emptied beginning in 1944, Americans of Japanese descent reaped a bitter harvest. They reentered society only to face vicious and continuing racism. Most were relocated elsewhere in the United States, outside exclusion zones, but the few who did return to the towns from which they'd been removed learned the family heirlooms they'd put in storage had been stolen, their land seized for unpaid taxes which they could not pay due to having been incarcerated against their will, or that strangers had moved into their homes.[37]

Not until 1980 did Congress take any steps to make restitution to the surviving Japanese Americans who had lost so much as a result of the Internment program, and then only begrudgingly. Over the next eight years, three rounds of bills were proposed to offer belated reparations to the 60,000 surviving internees: $20,000 per survivor and an official apology. Heirs of deceased internees received nothing.[38]

Talking About It

What makes discussions about race and racism so tough in America is that we're often far too confident in the clarity of our own personal lenses. If I entered conversations under the assumption that my experience is normative for all groups in this

---

[36] I encourage you to learn about life inside these camps. The details, which I will not take the time to recount here, are quite shocking.

[37] Ibid., 61.

[38] Ibid., 64.

country, I'd be operating from a massively underinformed stance.

As we've just noted, Asian-American immigrants contemporary with my grandfather experienced a different America than he did. As a Swedish immigrant who entered the country at a very young age, once he learned English, he was able to shed the externals of his immigrant status and blend in with natural-born citizens. Note that his acceptance hinged on his ability to assimilate into what was considered the norm. Though he was not a natural-born citizen, when he rose to defend American shores during World War II, no one questioned his national identity or loyalty. Regardless of his internal motivations, he was perceived in a positive light because, according to the prevailing wisdom of the day, his features marked him as a hero and not a traitor. Japanese immigrants were treated very differently. Mockery of their appearance and motives was so commonplace that it appeared in popular political cartoons.[39]

This didn't occur that long ago. My grandfather was alive to have witnessed these cartoons running in the paper, though it is too late now for me to ask him if he remembers seeing them. He died when I was still in my twenties. The threads of our shared past still run through the fabric of the present, and its effects on those who have gone before us ripple down through generations.

Every time I hear people make blanket statements that "America isn't racist" and "the real problem is that people can't move on," I want to start asking questions about how they've

---

[39] Fiona Macdonald, "The Surprisingly Radical Politics of Dr. Seuss." *BBC Culture.* March 2, 2019. https://www.bbc.com/culture/article/20190301-the-surprisingly-radical-politics-of-dr-seuss (Accessed February 9, 2021).

reached that conclusion. If the details in this chapter weren't enough, we could explore the African American experience with chattel slavery, Jim Crow, convict leasing, and the fight for Civil Rights. We could unpack the realities of North America's Indigenous population.

As I mentioned at the outset of this chapter, the issues of race in America are anything but black and white.

The "Well Actually" Girl who lives in my brain agrees with me on this. At a moment's notice, she's ready to strap on her parachute, reaching for her megaphone. I've learned over time, however, that this isn't the most effective way to handle these awkward topics.

I've found that instead of following my natural instincts and dropping from the sky spouting impassioned historical monologues, the best first step is often to slow down and shift my focus—especially when dealing with questions of race, racism, and racial justice. After all, when we use the terms *race* and *racist,* we might not even be talking about the same concepts.

Define Terms

What you and your conversation partner believe racism is and is not will have a lot to do with how well you're able to understand one another. If you're thinking of racism simply in terms of overtly racist acts such as joining hate groups, spray-painting swastikas on walls, and using racial slurs, and your conversation partner is thinking of things like the generational impacts of federal legislation or the effects of unconscious bias, of course you're going to find yourselves at odds conversationally. To make sure you're understanding one another from the outset, be sure to define your terms first. The conversation will most certainly still be awkward and fraught with potential landmines, but this simple first step will go a long way toward moving you toward a more productive outcome.

Ask Questions

When you think about asking questions, you might picture a fast-paced back and forth, like the conversational equivalent of ping-pong. In ping-pong, the focus is to react to an opponent's play as quickly as possible while simultaneously trying to get the ball past them. To win in ping-pong, we must stay in constant motion, the entirety of our focus combative and reactionary. In our conversations, the ping-pong method rarely results in meaningful dialogue.

That's because when we adopt a ping-pong mentality in difficult conversations about things like race, we can become overly focused on keeping track of when it's our turn to talk and what we're going to say. While we may feel that we're doing our part by providing a healthy give-and-take, what we're often seeking to do is pivot the conversation back to our own perspective as soon as possible. Thus, we speak without taking adequate time to understand the other person's position and what's shaped it. Such rapid-fire responses rarely strike at the heart of what the other person is actually trying to communicate. In our haste to respond, we're merely hitting back point by point, skimming the surface. The results of such conversations are seldom satisfying to either party.

If you suspect you're prone to playing conversational ping pong, here's my challenge. When someone makes a statement that activates your "Well Actually" response, see if you can go at least five steps through the conversation before you unleash your own inner "Well Actually" persona. While you may not be able to keep her from strapping on her parachute, you can choose not to let her jump out of the airplane just yet.

When I say you must go five steps through the conversation before the "Well Actually" Girl is unleashed, I mean let the person finish sentences and complete thoughts before responding. Then when you do respond, offer an intensifying comment or ask a clarifying question instead of diving in with your opinion, pushback, or rebuttal. The goal is to make sure you're understanding them fully and grasping the big picture of what they're saying before you seek to weigh in.

Try for more open-ended questions than ones that only require yes-no responses.

- "Interesting. Tell me more."
- "What has been your experience with this?"
- "How long have you thought this way?"
- "What changed your mind?"
- "I'd love to know what books you've read and/or who you listen to on this topic."
- "Why do you think this issue sparks such strong responses in people?"

Your responses don't have to be these exact five, of course.

Use ones that naturally suit the moment and your own personality. Just make it a goal to attempt five questions or intensifying statements in a row before you consider weighing in with your own thoughts. And don't think you're tricking anybody with a "Do you think so? Because I don't." That doesn't count.

Not only will this method broaden the scope of the conversation and help you build trust with the other person, but it'll also keep you from monopolizing the conversation, jumping in too quickly, or preemptively responding to things the other person hasn't said and may not even think, which is my own personal Achilles heel. In committing to at least five conversational exchanges before raising our own views, we're working against our hardwired reactive response. Instead of playing ping-pong with our conversations, we want to approach them more like we would a game of Scrabble.

The Scrabble Mentality

When approaching awkward conversations with a Scrabble mentality, we're still interested in presenting our own information; but we're much less reactive. We're free to take our time, observe the board, look down at what we have in our tray, and consider how best to present our information based on what the other person has already built. In Scrabble, it's not necessary to show all our tiles at once, nor is it wise. Throughout the game, we lay down only the letters that are needed, and only when they're called for. As we pass turns from one to another, we allow others plenty of time to think and make their moves—and our partners generally allow us the same luxury. We do challenge one another's word choice from time to time—but challenging is a risk that can backfire, so we're judicious about our challenges and only employ them when we're absolutely positive we're right.

While ping-pong communication is purely oppositional, with the first player to reach a set number of points winning the round, Scrabble communication is more collaborative. While we clearly disagree and would like eventually to hold the prevailing view, we're working together to build the board—a board from which we'll both benefit.

With this mindset in place at the start of awkward conversations, we're more likely to listen well and ask clarifying questions without feeling that we're losing a chance to score quick points. In doing so, we're better able to respond effectively to what our partners are actually saying. We don't get tunnel vision on one particular response, knowing that the board could change at any time, and we must adjust accordingly.

While our underlying main goal in these awkward conversations might still be to win our conversation partners over to our way of thinking, we must understand that this outcome is not always possible—nor, dare I say, even advisable. Few of us are experts on everything. If we're willing to engage in tough topics, we must approach most of them with at least a partial assumption that occasionally we will be the ones who have—up until this point—been wrong, misinformed, or underinformed. Therefore, individual conversations should be less about winning an argument and more about building stronger bridges of communication with our discussion partners.

Let It Burn

Yes, there may eventually come times to burn bridges. When people are obviously abusing our trust, acting in bad faith, or have proven themselves disingenuous, there's cause to disengage and cut off dialogue, at least for a time. But in recent years, I've seen too many people cutting others out of their lives over differences of opinion and simple disagreements. Over one awkward conversation turned disastrous. Rather than coming back and doing the hard work of mending fences by hashing through the tall weeds together in pursuit of a clear view for both sides, it seems many would rather disengage, retreat, and avoid each other indefinitely. While we'll eventually discuss how to deal with truly toxic conversation partners, for now, let's assume we're dealing with good-faith conversations partners and evaluate the mentality with which we approach awkward topics in such situations, especially ones related to race and racism in America.

I'm a little ashamed to tell you that I'm a newer participant in these conversations. Up until a few years ago, I wouldn't have touched these topics with a ten-foot pole. Recently, however, as both my knowledge and compassion for others have grown, I've become convicted that I've been wrong to avoid it all this time just to spare myself potential hurt, pain, and unpleasantness. To avoid pain at the expense of others is, in many ways, the antithesis of the way of Jesus Christ. While his life modeled pain and mortal self-sacrifice for the benefit of others, I could barely bring myself to endure temporary awkwardness.

The change in me has been gradual; and during the shift, I've made a lot of mistakes along the way, including expending far too much energy parachuting in as the "Well Actually" Girl. Now that I've learned to slow down, ask questions, and focus on taking my time, I'm both learning more and communicating more effectively. It's a blessing. It's also still a struggle. It's an awkward conversation, after all, and those will never be easy—but valuable endeavors rarely are.

What Holds Us Back

One of my Facebook connections recently sent me an article about Seneca Village. Located in New York, in the 19th century, Seneca Village was home to a thriving and diverse community of predominantly African American property owners. The village supported its own institutions, including three churches, five cemeteries, and a school. When a group of prominent New York City residents began pushing for a grand uptown park in the 1840s, the City government claimed the land under the right of eminent domain, evicted its residents, razed their homes and businesses, and made way for what is now New York's Central Park.[40] What's interesting to me today is not so much that my Facebook connection shared this article. She's known for sharing articles, memes, and images she finds interesting or thinks might engage her followers. It's that she shared this one only with me—and through private messenger, at that.

---

[40] "Seneca Village Project." Columbia University. http://projects.mcah.columbia.edu/seneca_village/htm/history.htm (Accessed February 17, 2021).

In one sense, I don't blame her. Social media is one of the more toxic spaces in which you could find yourself embroiled in discussions related to race. In another sense, I couldn't help but notice how out of character this move is for her. Why be so public about everything else she shares and yet so private about this? What happened in Seneca is straight-up historical fact. What's holding her back from sharing this article with the rest of her friends and family members on social media? I suspect it's the same thing that holds many of us back in similar situations.

- Fear of being attacked for your beliefs/stance.
- Fear of saying the wrong thing.
- Fear of being misrepresented.
- Fear of being misunderstood.
- Fear of your dentist and your best friend from third grade getting into a fight in your comments.

All of these fears can easily paralyze us into inaction; yet while these fears may never really abate, we shouldn't let them hold us back from pressing forward to engage tough and awkward conversations around these issues. There's just too much at stake.

What We Lose

When we're either unwilling or unable to engage in the tough topic of race and racism, we are in danger of breaking the second of the greatest commandments: that of loving our neighbors as ourselves.[41] In reflecting on the Parable of the Good Samaritan, Tim Keller makes this important note about the greater context of Jesus' teaching that day:

> When Jesus is asked to define love of neighbor, he depicts someone who, at great risk and sacrifice, meets the physical and material needs of a man of a different race and religion from himself (Luke 10:25-37). "Go and do likewise," Jesus says to us, meaning that we must treat people of other races, nationalities, classes, and groups with the same amount of care, respect, and love that we would give to ourselves or members of our own communities.[42]

On this basis, it is incumbent on Christians to work actively against racial injustice both inside and outside the church. It's not enough just not to be racist. We must be actively anti-racist. For me, on the very lowest level, that started with conversations in my own community.

Yes, these conversations are awkward. They require us to push past that feeling in order to engage. But they require more than that.

---

[41] Mark 12:28-34.
[42] Timothy Keller. "The Sin of Racism." *Life in the Gospel*. https://quarterly.gospelinlife.com/the-sin-of-racism/ (Accessed February 17, 2021).

Taking Time

It takes courage to speak up about any controversial issue. Racism especially so. Here in the United States, people have strong opinions on the matter and often become quickly upset if you don't immediately agree with them. Even when we're loving and careful in our approach, such conversations can prove costly. At the very least, they consume a lot of time—time most of us would rather be doing something else. Think of what you'd rather be doing than hammering out the definition of racism with Uncle Bob. Probably literally anything.

It's worth the reminder here that defining your terms with your communication partner can spare you both a layer of frustration. These conversations require patience, a hard virtue when so much of the time we are naturally impatient. They're emotionally taxing, and we're all on edge. And nearly always, all parties involved are open to confusion, frustration, and anger as a direct result. It's no wonder most of us would avoid it if we can.

We must make time for these conversations, however. For one thing, if you don't speak up about Uncle Bob's racist assumptions, someone else down the road will have to do it. Why purposefully leave that job to others?

As a Christian, I believe the gospel provides a blueprint for our entire lives. In Jesus, we see someone bearing an undeserved weight so that we do not have to bear it. If I walk in his steps, I'm willing to take on undeserved and unwanted tasks in order to spare others from having to bear them.

Furthermore, even if a conversation doesn't go exactly as I

plan, it can still have a positive effect. Sometimes sustained effort over time is exactly what's needed for change to come. Think of the difference between flipping on a kitchen light and waiting for the gym lights to warm up. Some changes are quick. Others are gradual. In tackling tough topics like race and racism, sometimes people need time to stretch, learn, grow, and adjust after decades of static thinking. For their pupils to constrict and their gaze to sharpen as their eyes are opened to the light.

Let's not give up too soon. It's worth it to press forward and engage tough topics. Even when we feel socially awkward.

Starting with Yourself

If you're not sure where to start, you can always start with yourself. Jemar Tisby, the author of *How to Fight Racism,* believes that exploring your own racial identity can help you find a pathway into these conversations. By delving into your own family's past and present views and experiences with race, you not only learn more about how your context has shaped you, but you open natural pathways into honest conversations. It's wise to prepare yourself spiritually and emotionally before embarking on this path, Tisby warns, because what you find may shock, sadden, or anger you. In other cases, you may be encouraged by the patterns you uncover. Either way, investigating your family's individual ethnicity and learning how your family members interacted with those around them is a foundational practice that can root you more deeply in your own context. Such an investigation can also help you find a way to begin discussing matters related to race and racism with those closest to you.[43]

> Be honest about your purpose. Tell people you are trying to understand your racial history and identity better, and to do that you want to understand how the people who influenced you think about such topics. The goal is to gather information, not necessarily to tell them what you think.
>
> Use open-ended questions such as, "What was it like growing up in your family?" or "What do you remember about what was happening in your town when you were a teenager?"
>
> Listen without offering your own analysis or judgment. Even if you find the stories repugnant or painful, your willingness to listen will encourage more conversation.[44]

I found this practice helpful in my own life. On several occasions, my parents have been willing to discuss racial crisis points from their past: the Civil Rights Movement, during which time they both lived in downtown Chicago, and the Vietnamese Refugee Resettlement of the late 70's, an event that directly impacted the area where we lived when I was a small child.

---

[43] Jemar Tisby. *How to Fight Racism: Courageous Christianity and the Journey toward Racial Justice.* (Grand Rapids: Zondervan Reflective, 2021), 54.
[44] Ibid, 55.

The past is gone. None of us can re-live it. For those who are dealing with regrets, this reality may cause pain. Beyond the pain, however, is the possibility for redemption, growth, and the potential for change. If our awkward conversations can create more fertile soil for growth in these areas, then is it not worth it to press through discomfort to engage tough topics?

Hope for the Future

The threads of the past run through the fabric of the present, and how we understand the past informs how we process life now. In discussing the most recent events that unfolded in 2020 and 2021, you'd have to go out of your way *not* to talk about race. If that's you, I'm not here to shame you. I'm here to remind you that it's not too late to start. Take the lessons of this chapter to heart, spend some time in prayer, screw your courage to the sticking place, and go engage in some awkward conversations.

From the Ashes

What if you've already crashed and burned on these topics? What if you've already shut down so many conversations that no one will engage you anymore? Your response shouldn't be to backpedal entirely.

The beauty of the gospel is that nothing and no one is beyond hope, repair, repentance, or renewal. Our Father is on the throne, Jesus is alive at his right hand, and the Spirit is at work in the world. Throughout recorded Scripture and in our daily lives, we've been able to witness broken relationships restored, shipwrecked lives renewed, and hearts forever changed. Our God truly brings beauty from ashes. He does so on personal, societal, global, and cosmic scales. If he can hold the cosmos together, he can hold you together while you tackle tough topics.

Flip the Script

A few years ago, I heard a Korean American Christian leader say something that stuck with me. In describing how Asian-Americans have sometimes been leveraged as ideological wedges between other ethnic communities, Raymond Chang, a professor at Wheaton College, pointed out God's power to flip Satan's scheme on its head.

Though Satan desires to leverage racism to drive people apart, Chang reminded us that wedges can serve another purpose. When pivoted, wedges can be transformed into ramps.[45] When we rely on the Spirit for help, conversations that could easily drive wedges between us can become ramps to glorify God and proclaim the gospel of Jesus Christ.

---

[45] Raymond Chang in "The Gospel in the Asian American Experience" 1:05:16 https://www.thegospelcoalition.org/conference_media/gospel-asian-american-experience/ (Accessed December 28, 2019). Specifically, he was discussing the way in which Asian Americans, as "Model Minorities," are often leveraged against African Americans.

Start Your Own Awkward Conversation

Find some trusted conversation partners for discussion or consider the questions on your own.

1. In what way can ethnic heritage influence different aspects of the American experience? How can this dynamic affect our conversations surrounding race and racism in America?

2. Why are conversations surrounding issues of race often so challenging?

3. What most holds you back from addressing the topics of race and racism? Alternately, if you speak out often, what motivates you?

4. Consider the statement from Raymond Chang: "Wedges can be transformed into ramps." What are the implications of this statement?

5. What could we gain by pressing through discomfort to engage socially awkward conversations regarding race and racism? What do we miss by avoiding them?

Welcome to Awkwardsville:
Now Accepting Compliments

For a time, I spent every Sunday going out to lunch with my sister Bethany and our friend Pam. On one such recent meal, after we'd eaten and stood to leave, we found ourselves exiting the restaurant next to a family. The husband and wife were dressed tidily, as were their teenage children.

As we held the doors for one another, the mom sidled up next to Bethany and me and leaned in close. "You two are just so stylish." She grinned and pursed her lips together, looking us up and down. Given the way her eyes lingered, she obviously approved of Bethany's slim dress and tall heels. She also gave an approving nod to my floaty black top and fitted capris. Stopping in the door, she let her gaze travel from the tips of my sandaled toes to the top of my flyaway pixie cut. "I wish I had hair like yours. And really," she gestured up and down, "just this whole look. I'm jealous."

Bethany thanked her for her part of the compliment, sliding on a pair of sunglasses and stepping onto the sidewalk.

I smiled and said thanks but felt the need to protest. She was being so kind, but I was living a lie. "Oh, you have nothing to be jealous of. I basically got this whole outfit at a thrift store. These pants were only seven dollars. And look," I bent my right leg at the knee and lifted it, stork-like, to bring my ankle more in range with her line of sight. "The stitching's coming out of this cuff, and it fell out this morning. I had to tuck it back up and hope it stayed, which so far it has."

She took a breath to reply, but I was still going. She had to know it all.

"Oh, and these shoes are, like, thirteen years old. I got them for my sister's wedding. Not that sister—the other one, who lives in Georgia. That's how I know exactly how old they are, because her twins are twelve now."

"Well, okay . . . I still think you look great." The kind woman with the compliments headed one direction, while Pam, Bethany, and I headed the other.

Bethany had the decency to wait until she was out of earshot. "Ruth. Repeat after me."

"Repeat what?" I waved goodbye to our new friend.

"When someone gives you a compliment, you just have to say, 'Thank you.'"

CHAPTER 4
Let's Talk About Sex

"The talk," we call it. *The* talk. As if one conversation is enough to teach children everything they'll ever need to know about sexual relationships and human reproduction. Now that I'm middle aged, I've watched plenty of my friends writhe about this phase of child-rearing. I know it's stressful for parents, and I understand why. I'm sure my parents felt the same. But if they ever actually gave me "the talk," I certainly don't remember it. This doesn't mean they didn't do a good job. My mom says she had a little booklet she took each of us through. But whatever was said, my brain has jettisoned the memory. This doesn't mean I consider them bad parents or neglectful in any way. In fact, in this matter, my parents are statistically average.

By the Numbers

From the introduction to this book, you've already seen the statistics about how little sex is discussed between parents and children. Based on my memory, sex must have been discussed in my home seldom or hardly ever.

To be honest, I heard way more messages about sex at school than I did at home. And I'm not just talking about whispers and rumors about who had done it or was currently doing it. I'm talking instead about the discourse we heard directly from our authority figures.

The Fundamentals of Sex

For a number of years, my siblings and I attended a small Christian high school that was part of the Independent Fundamental Baptist movement. Our family wasn't part of the denomination ourselves, but as I look back now, I recognize that my spiritual formation was heavily influenced by the messages I received there.[46] Though it was never stated in so many words, the perception I developed over the six years I attended that school was that sex is bad and dangerous. Good kids not only avoided having sex, but they also avoided talking about sex because anyone who talked about, thought about, or joked about sex was perverted and dirty. Scripture told us to keep our minds on higher things.

Our chapel speakers would generally dispense with the role of sex within marriage in a single sentence or two. "Sex is intended for marriage." After which they would preach on the perils of sex outside marriage with impassioned monologues filled with dire warnings and fiery pronouncements about what would happen to

---

[46] I discuss this dynamic a bit in more detail in my book *The Cross in the Culture: Connecting Our Stories to the Greatest Story Ever Told*, Build a Better Us, 2020.

anyone who had premarital sex. During this time, if any of them ever cast a positive vision for the proper role of sex in the grand scheme of things, I don't remember it.

When I say I heard more about sex in school than at home, I include not just the conversations we had with our parents but also any media we consumed. Though I remember authority figures being concerned about what my generation was absorbing from "the world," my contact with society's cultural touchstones was vastly more limited than what's available today. I came of age before internet use was really a thing, which meant my media consumption at the time was largely through print, TV, and the occasional movie. While our family did own a television, we weren't big TV watchers. We did watch the nightly news. If it touched on the sexual, it generally did so in more veiled terms than are used today. Although when the John and Lorena Bobbitt story broke in 1993, I learned a lot.

A Sex-Saturated Society

I grew up hearing that America is a sex-saturated society, and eventually I encountered evidence for myself. The amount of sexual content that appears in our cultural artifacts (books, movies, TV shows, music), coupled with the way sex is talked about freely in the public square shocked me. Never mind the rising tide of porn use and the rampant sexual exploitation of vulnerable children, women, and men.[47] Whether art is influencing life, life influencing art, or a potent mixture of the two, America's sexual landscape has shifted dramatically over the last few decades, bringing sex to the forefront of public conversations in ways I haven't witnessed in my lifetime.

Anecdotal evidence and subjective opinion are one matter; but statistics also bear this out. According to a study published this decade, generational changes—coupled with a rising tide of individualism—demonstrate continuing fruit of the Sexual Revolution:

- Between the 1970s and the 2010s, American adults became more accepting of premarital sex, adolescent sex, and same-sex activity, but less accepting of extramarital sex.
- In the early 1970s, 29% of Americans believed that premarital sex was not wrong at all. This rose to around 42% in the 1980s and stayed there through the 1990s, rising to 49% in the 2000s and to 55% in the 2010s.
- Among Boomers who were eighteen to twenty-nine years old in the 1970s, 47% believed premarital sex was not wrong at all. In the 1990s, 50% of Gen X'ers who were the same age agreed, as did 62% of Millennials in the

---

[47] Seventy-three percent of the world's online pornography is produced in the United States. A staggering statistic. Judith Mackay, NCBI, "How does the United States compare with the rest of the world in human sexual behavior?" https://www.ncbi.nlm.nih.gov/pmc/articles/PMC1071438/ (Accessed July 3, 2020).

2010s.

- Something similar can be said of same-sex activity, with 21% of the Boomers in the early 1970s who were between eighteen to twenty-nine years old stating it was not wrong at all. At the same age in the 1990s, 26% of Gen X'ers said the same, and 56% of Millennials in the 2010s agreed.
- The total number of sexual partners since age eighteen increased from seven in the late 1980s to eleven in the 2010s.
- Among eighteen to twenty-nine-year-olds reporting non-partner sex, 35% of Gen X'ers in the late 1980s had sex with a casual date or pickup, compared to 45% of Millennials in the 2010s.[48]

Viewpoints relating to sex and sexuality are shifting on massive scales, pulling our children along. Adolescents are having more sex at younger ages than my peers did. And yet in many Christian households, we're simply not talking about it—any of it.

Unwillingness or inability to talk frankly about issues related to sex and sexuality aren't just issues that affect our children, however. It is affecting all of us.

---

[48] Twenge, J.M., Sherman, R.A. & Wells, B.E. Changes in American Adults' Sexual Behavior and Attitudes, 1972–2012. *Arch Sex Behav* 44, 2273–2285 (2015). https://doi.org/10.1007/s10508-015-0540-2 (Accessed July 3, 2020).

Talking About Sex

I know talking about sex and sexuality can be awkward. I'm not denying that. I speak from personal experience. As a single and celibate woman, I feel extra awkward talking about sex. Yet people like me need these conversations as much as anybody.

I have a question for the other singles reading along: If you're also single and grappling with issues related to lust, sexual longings and temptation, masturbation, or celibacy, where would you be comfortable bringing such topics up for discussion, support, advice, and prayer? In your Bible study group? With your mentor? With a trusted Christian friend? Who are your in-person conversation partners regarding sex and sexuality? We all need them. A lack of personal, in-person encouragements in these areas can make a huge difference.

I spoke to a young woman recently who confided that she'd heard so many dire warnings and chastisements that she was actually so afraid of sex she wasn't sure she ever wanted to get married. What followed was a very fruitful conversation, one that likely would never have come about as a result of a youth group session, sermon series, podcast, YouTube video, blog post, or article. It was only through an open and vulnerable one-on-one conversation—and a very awkward one, at that—that we were able to establish the sort of rapport that would even allow those issues to come to the surface.

Of course, singles aren't the only ones who need to talk about sex. If you're married and struggling in your sex life, who can you talk to? Does your small group address these topics? Are your mentors open to these topics? Who would be a safe conversation partner with whom you can bring up the fact that you're lonely in your marriage? That you haven't had sex with your spouse in over six months? That sex is physically painful or emotionally stressful, but you don't know how to address it?

A few years ago, I was talking to some married friends of mine about these exact issues. We'd just finished eating dinner and were lounging in the living room enjoying a post-pasta haze. This couple was about two years into their marriage at the time, and one of them made the comment that one thing he hadn't been prepared for was that even within marriage, "Sex is weird and hard to navigate, and nobody's really talking about it."

He's right, at least in the circles in which I travel. Though I'm fairly unflappable and mostly open to awkward conversations, I haven't often been privy to open discussion of sex or sexual problems of any variety. That includes not only the issues I listed above but also matters relating to sexual abuse and assault. The consequences of not talking about those subjects are heavy, and we will discuss them in more detail in Chapter 11.

For now, let's explore why we have so much trouble talking about these matters, what that says about us, and how we can help shift the conversation into healthier channels.

Why Are We Like This?

To understand why we have so much trouble talking about sex and sexuality, perhaps we should start by taking a step back and looking at the big picture. In Ephesians 5, we see that the marriage union is given to us as a picture of Christ's union with the church. By extension, marriage, sex, and sexuality are not given as ends in themselves but as avenues by which we can understand what it means to be made in the image of a Triune God and experience an echo of the divine union.

We are made in the image of a God who is an all-sufficient, three-in-one being. By contrast, we are only one. Because of this gap between our essence and our expectations, we experience a deep need for connection and intimacy. This is just as true for those who do not acknowledge their Creator as it is for those who do. Deep down, we all know we cannot make it on our own—nor do we want to try. In God's plan, we all need one another. Though at different points some need more and some need less, we all need each other, and strange things happen when people are left alone too long. Look at Tom Hanks in *Castaway*. Look at the rest of us during pandemic lockdowns. Look at solitary confinement.

Human beings were not created with the intention that they spend twenty-three hours of each day in deep and echoing solitude—and it shows. According to a study published by the *Journal of the American Academy of Psychiatry and the Law*, the correlation between solitary confinement in the prison system and mental illness among incarcerated people should raise serious ethical questions—questions that go straight to the core of what it means to be human.

> Solitary confinement is recognized as difficult to withstand; indeed, psychological stressors such as isolation can be as clinically distressing as

> physical torture . . . Isolation can be psychologically harmful to any prisoner, with the nature and severity of the impact depending on the individual, the duration, and particular conditions such as access to natural light, books, or radio. Psychological effects can include anxiety, depression, anger, cognitive disturbances, perceptual distortions, obsessive thoughts, paranoia, and psychosis.[49]

Unsurprisingly, suicides occur disproportionately more often in segregation units than any other place in prison.[50] This is a heartbreaking reality, and one that should speak in a special way to Christians. As God affirmed at the creation of Adam, it is not good for us to be alone.[51] When God placed the first people in the Garden of Eden, they lived in constant fellowship with Him and with each other. This is the way we were meant to experience the world.

If you're familiar with the creation account in Genesis, you know that when God said it was not good for man to be alone, those words were spoken within the Godhead between the creation of the first man, Adam, and the first woman, Eve. There's a lot that could be said about being made in the image of God, but what

---

[49] Jeffrey L. Metzner and Jamie Fellner, "Solitary Confinement and Mental Illness in U.S. Prisons: A Challenge for Medical Ethics," *The Journal of the American Academy of Psychiatry and the Law 38* (March 2010), http://jaapl.org/content/38/1/104 (Accessed July 28, 2020).
[50] Ibid.
[51] Genesis 2:18.

matters for the purpose of our current discussion is that we realize the limits of what that means.[52] God is self-existent, self-sustaining, and self-perpetuating. We are not. We are created beings, kept alive by the pleasure of his will. One way we show our lack is in our basic needs for relational connections—since, unlike God, we cannot provide those within ourselves. In God's plan, we are designed to need him and one another. To rely on others is not weakness but a way in which we become stronger and more whole.

Our deep need for intimacy is only a weakness to the extent that we abuse, misuse, and misunderstand it. At its best, our need drives us to find its right and natural fulfillment in healthy relationships with God and one another. At its worst, our need drives us to misuse our relational gifts—including sex.

Being Intimate

As we have already established, I came of age in a Christian subculture. Apart from parents having "the talk" with their children and pastors preaching sermons warning against fornication, it seemed to me that "good Christians" avoided talking about sex altogether. To my recollection, no one talked in any significant way about why God gave us sex in the first place, what it signified, and how it was merely a shadow—a foretaste—of the joy we will experience when in total and complete union with him.

---

[52] A simple and clear book outlining this point in more detail is Jen Wilkin's 2016 book *None Like Him: 10 Ways God Is Different from Us (and Why That's a Good Thing)*.

Though I can't speak for everyone, during my research for my book on singleness and the church, I talked to enough of my peers to understand that my experience was fairly common.[53] For most of us, sex wasn't talked about freely, and if we raised any questions about it, we were likely to be given a book or a resource to read instead of a personal conversation. As you can imagine, the helpfulness of such resources can vary widely. And although such books were sometimes accompanied with an invitation to follow up with any questions after reading the book, the very fact that we were handed a resource rather than invited into conversation from the outset sent a subtle, discouraging message.

When talking about sex absolutely couldn't be avoided, any mention was shrouded in mystery and innuendo. *Intimacy,* it was usually called, or *marital relations.* I will spare you the complete list of euphemisms. This led me to believe not only that we couldn't talk about sex but that we shouldn't name it.

In her excellent work *Talking Back to Purity Culture,* author Rachel Joy Welcher discusses this dynamic: "Our choice to detach the topic of sexual purity from regular conversation has isolated it from the whole of Scripture and life, turning questions that are meant to press us further into prayer, the church, and God's Word into books, conferences, and websites. But the subject of sexual purity is too nuanced to squeeze into one book or conference. It must be integrated into our regular conversations."[54]

---

[53] Ruth Buchanan. *The Proper Care and Feeding of Singles: How Pastors, Marrieds, and Church Leaders Effectively Support Solo Members, Write Integrity Press, 2017.*
[54] Rachel Joy Welcher. *Talking Back to Purity Culture: Rediscovering Faithful Christian Sexuality.* (Downers Grove: InterVarsity Press, 2020), 12.

Why Does It Matter?

Why does any of this matter? Should we really be out here talking about sex all the time in front of God and everybody, including our children? I say yes—and we shouldn't be using euphemisms.

I've heard sex called all kinds of things—some of which are funny, others of which are rude, and all of which I'm not going to repeat here, mostly because they're silly. Some euphemisms, however, actually cause harm. This harm may be unintentional, but that doesn't stop it from having an effect.

Take, for example, calling sex *intimacy*. In my experience, this has been by far the number one replacement I've heard deployed in my little pocket of American Christianity. But sex and intimacy aren't the same thing, and we have two different words to represent them for a reason. You can have sex without intimacy and intimacy without sex.

Treating the words *sex* and *intimacy* as if they're synonymous leads to a powerful misrepresentation to both concepts. As someone who's gone through rather lonely stretches of celibate adult singlehood, I'm especially sensitive to their conflation. While I expect society to tell me I must have sex in order to enjoy intimate connections with other people, I don't expect people in the church to mirror the messaging—yet they do so unconsciously by using the words *sex* and *intimacy* as if they are interchangeable.

I've written extensively elsewhere on the relational clash of long-term singleness and how well-meaning church members sometimes compound the challenges of single life.[55] I will not reiterate any of that here. For now, I will simply point out that when we equate sex with intimacy, we may be subconsciously pushing people toward a position we don't even hold. We're also unknowingly reinforcing the message that if people are going to reach important levels of intimate human connection, they'll be required to have sex. That's just not true.

Speaking as someone who's not currently having sex, equating sex with intimacy actually gives sex a greater attraction than it already has. If sex equals intimacy, sex could become the balm that will, theoretically, not only soothe my passions and lusts but perhaps also fulfill my deep and aching relational needs. If I equate intimacy with sex, then sex becomes the single object by which I can obtain it. By requiring faithful chastity from me, God would then be cutting me off from the very object for which I'm created: meaningful connection.

Of course, he's done no such thing.

We can maintain meaningful connections and exist in deep and intimate relationships without having sex. At least, we should. And for proof, we need look no further than Jesus.

Jesus Knows

In her book *Party of One,* author Joy Beth Smith writes that contemplating Jesus' sexuality made her feel "closer to Jesus-the-man" than she had in a while.

---

[55] Buchanan, *The Proper Care and Feeding of Singles.*

Jesus had to navigate his way through sexuality as well—he had to figure out his body and control its reactions as a young boy and later as an adult, even as women knelt at his feet or tugged on his robes. He had to establish his boundaries, keeping unhealthy people far outside his inner sanctum as he tried to develop healthy rhythms. He cultivated intimacy with others, including his twelve disciples and a select group of women, and in doing all that, his sexuality was running in the background, just as ours does every day.[56]

I love that imagery—of sexuality running like a background operation. It closely aligns with my experience, but it wasn't something I'd thought much about in terms of Jesus' incarnate time. Like Smith, I find it comforting to know that Jesus knows how I'm feeling. He lived as a sexual being with innate instincts and desires. He maintained meaningful, intimate connections with the people in his life who were closest to him. And he lived and died as a chaste, fully whole, never-married man. It was a comfort I didn't realize I needed until I found it.

---

[56] Joy Beth Smith. *Party of One: Truth, Longing, and the Subtle Art of Singleness* (Nashville: Thomas Nelson, 2018) 93-94.

What We Lose

Through Smith's study, my perceptions of Jesus' life experience have deepened significantly. I had never before contemplated what it means that Jesus was a healthy single man with a sex drive. Therefore, it never occurred to me how well-suited he was as a confidante and ally in my singleness.

These are precisely the sorts of realizations we lose when we fail to factor sex and sexuality into our discussions. In keeping silent on matters of sex and sexuality, we're closing ourselves off to opportunities to care for one another holistically. In my case, I'm a middle-aged single woman practicing celibacy. Those who do not take those aspects of my experience into consideration will not see me was a whole person. What I've found is that many people would prefer to think of single Christian women like me either as repressed sex maniacs bent on tempting men and stealing husbands, or as purely sexless beings born to teach Sunday School and sing in the choir with never a hormone to disturb a solid night's sleep. And if we never talk about sex, everyone's free to rest in these assumptions.

And I'm left wrestling with my problems alone.

But that's not the worst of what we lose. In keeping silent on matters of sex and sexuality—particularly in front of our children—we're ceding authority in those areas to anyone who's willing to take up the mantle and talk about it. For many children, that will be their peers. For some, it will be people at work and school. For others, it will be the internet. Or a predator—heaven help us. Our children need us to overcome our awkwardness and meet them where they are, answering their questions and affirming their very natural curiosity about sex. They need to hear the truth, both at home and at church.

Most churches don't keep totally silent on matters of sex and sexuality. However, mentions of both seem reserved either for the pulpit or for niche groups (youth group "purity" talks, for instance[57]). This is not the way it's supposed to be.

The First (and Last) Word

As the inventor of sex, God should have the first and last say in the matter—and don't worry, he does. He uses Scripture, the ministry of the Holy Spirit, faithful mentors, and friends as he applies truth to our hearts and lives. By allowing him to speak through these avenues, we're opening ourselves to the richness of his whole spiritual counsel. The only question is whether we're open to having these conversations, willing both to listen and contribute.

This is not to say that we should talk about sex all the time with anybody who happens to be around. I do believe there should be some boundaries and privacy. But the fences we place around these topics should not be so high as to feel unassailable. As a general rule, if we're taking responsibility within our communities, *each of us* should be talking about these matters with somebody.

---

[57] Not that I'd recommend those unequivocally. Some have done a lot of damage. For more on this, see Rachel Welcher's excellent book *Talking Back to Purity Culture: Rediscovering Faithful Christian Sexuality,* InterVarsity Press, 2020.

Whether that means identifying a trusted conversation partner or becoming one for someone else, you are in the best position to judge. All I'm asking is that we no longer avoid the opportunity to foster meaningful dialogue around issues relating to sex and sexuality. There's too much at stake—too much we're all going to lose—if we leave these matters shrouded in silence.

What We Lose

When awkwardness causes us to avoid healthy and frank discussion of sex and sexuality in our relationships, homes, and churches, here are the opportunities we lose:

- Counseling and encouraging with lovingkindness.
- Learning from one another's personal experiences, positive or negative, and praising God for how he's brought sexual healing, restored relationships, and freedom from guilt and shame.
- Coming alongside those who are sexually struggling, tempted, hurt, or in need of healing.
- Seeking and offering support with prayer and compassion.
- Holding one another accountable.
- Correcting misconceptions and bringing Scripture to bear on the culture's ever-drifting sexual values.
- Confessing our faults to one another and praying for each other.

- Giving God the glory for how he's seen us through various sexual issues.

May today be the last day we let such opportunities pass us by.

Start Your Own Awkward Conversation

Find some trusted conversation partners for discussion or consider the questions on your own.

1. As a general rule, do you encourage or discourage open discussions involving sex or sexuality? In what ways?

2. In your opinion, who should be discussing issues of sex and sexuality together? Where might people look for their trusted conversation partners?

3. Can you think of a time an open discussion of sex and sexuality was helpful to you? Who were you talking to and why was it such a help?

4. Discuss your parents' or guardians' approach to teaching you about sex when you were growing up. What did they do well? What do you wish they'd done differently?

5. What can we gain by pressing through discomfort to

engage socially awkward conversations regarding sex and sexuality?

Socially Awkward

Welcome to Awkwardsville:
The Kicker

I'm sure we've all embarrassed ourselves at the gym at some point, but this was on another level. For a time, my sister Bethany and I worked out together in one of those sleek, colorful studios in which a group class rotates from rowing machines to treadmills to the weight floor, and the coach wears a headset mic. The walls are made of glass, through which the next batch of attendees lines up by the entry door stretching and watching our cooldown.

One morning while catching our collective breath after a particularly tough workout, Bethany and I were walking past our coach, funneling toward the exit door at the back, when my sister said something unexpected. I don't remember the exact words, but she was teasing me about my unsteady performance in one of the last sets. Since we'd recently told our coach that we used to kickbox together, I decided that the appropriate response to her sass would be to pause and mule-kick her. I was in no way concerned that I would hurt her. For one thing, I don't kick very hard. For another, I knew she would block it.

What I didn't know was that one of our classmates decided to sneak past us to the door in that very moment. Hearing a muffled "oof," I pivoted on my heel to see a tall, thin white man doubled forward, arms crossed low. I'd kicked him directly in the groin.

He bent at the waist, the brim of his cap blocking the expression on his face. I prayed for him to keep his head down. I had no desire to see him—neither his expression nor his actual face. If I knew exactly who I'd kicked, I'd never be able to go back to the gym again without fearing I'd be stuck on the rower directly next to the guy I'd inadvertently mule-kicked in the privates.

"I'm so sorry," I yelped. I may have patted his shoulder. Maybe not. It's all a blur. I asked Bethany recently to clarify this memory, and she has only the foggiest memories of it even happening. If only I were so lucky.

CHAPTER 5
Bearing the Weight

I'll never look like those women in magazine ads. And actually, neither will they.

By this point, we're all aware that the media pushes unrealistic body image expectations. Starting in mid-twentieth century darkrooms and continuing into the digital revolution unfolding in the current era, those already-stunning models and actors who grace our billboards and our screens have had their attractive points further amplified in one way or another. Tummies are tucked and dark eye circles erased. Blemishes and stretch marks are air-brushed away. "Bad" curves are sucked in, and "good" curves rounded out. Lighting and camera angles create a false softness and symmetry few experience, particularly not when gazing in horror at our own reflections in the mirrors of dressing room doors. Starting in the 1940s, slim or skinny bodies were presented as the norm. This changed in the 1980s, when an aerobics craze ushered in a new focus on fitness. Suddenly muscles were in. Through the 90's, "The Waif" was the standard, and Kate

Moss was held up as the norm.[58] My high school and college years played out during the 1990s, and I'm old enough to remember these trends developing before my eyes and the way in which people tried to hold the media accountable for the constant airbrushing and retouching.

"What will this do to our children?" people were asking. "Will seeing these doctored images set the bar too high?"

It was an important question—and still is. Our conceptions of our body images determine how we think and feel about ourselves, and by extension how we behave towards our bodies. Will we nourish them or starve them? Will we rest, work out, or punish ourselves? The complicated matrix of decisions surrounding how we treat our physical selves all connects back to how we perceive our bodies in relation to the bodies around us.

Who Sets the Standard?

A large part of our collective imagination is shaped by images appearing in print media, television, and on the big screen. Now, of course, we don't even need to get the professionals involved. With the technology available at our fingertips, we're able to retouch our own selfies in a matter of seconds. And we do—some of us more than others. Among teenage girls, in some contexts, photo retouching has become the new normal, with nine out of ten girls altering their images in some way before posting them to

---

[58] Katrina Pascual. "Body Positivity and Inclusivity in Marketing Campaigns." *Penji.* https://penji.co/body-positivity-marketing/ (Accessed March 10, 2021).

social media.[59]

Retouching ranges from relatively minor tweaks like whitening teeth, erasing blemishes, or smoothing wrinkles, to more dramatic modifications, such as elongating limbs, increasing breast sizes, altering skin tones, contouring eyes, slimming waists, and changing the shape and size of arms and thighs.

In response to this common practice, certain media outlets decided to flag obviously altered images. Ironically, further studies found that labeling these images as "manipulated" or "enhanced" can backfire, seeming only to increase the human desire to aspire to an unattainable ideal.

While each individual alteration may not seem like a big deal at the time, there's evidence that they have a cumulative effect.

Such studies have limitations in what they reveal, and the impact of images is dependent on social and cultural context. Still, the ubiquity of increasingly unrealistic digital images does feed into our beauty ideals and aspirations. It seems that we continue to hold digitally modified images as ideals even when we are told that they are not real. If this is the case, then simply providing information or knowledge is not sufficient.[60]

In other words, the solution to disordered body-image issues

---

[59] Rhiannon Lucy Cosslett, "Thinner, smoother, better: in the era of retouching, that's what girls have to be," *The Guardian* (September 8, 2016), https://www.theguardian.com/commentisfree/2016/sep/08/thinner-retouching-girls-image-manipulation-women (Accessed March 5, 2021).

[60] MacCallum F, Widdows H. Altered Images: Understanding the Influence of Unrealistic Images and Beauty Aspirations. *Health Care Anal.* 2018;26(3):235-245. doi:10.1007/s10728-016-0327-1 Access online: https://www.ncbi.nlm.nih.gov/pmc/articles/PMC6061013/ (Accessed March 5, 2021).

caused by unrealistic expectations isn't simply to inform a watching world that such images are manipulated. As this study concludes, beauty ideals are culturally constructed, and if they are to be challenged, they must be analyzed as any other cultural norm would be.[61]

This is where awkward conversations about body and body image issues can prove extremely productive.

A Weighty Matter

For decades now, we've witnessed evidence of society's pushback on unrealistic body-image expectations, particularly for women. Pushes for the "perfect" body are now met by both the Body Positivity and Fat Acceptance movements. While both have accomplished some good, neither has ultimately solved all the problems related to how we view and communicate about our bodies.

Body Positivity

"Body positivity is, by its very definition, about viewing our bodies as something that is not only perfectly acceptable but entirely wonderful," writes Stephanie Yeboah in *Vogue*. "In a world where the overriding mentality is that we should be ashamed of our bodies (particularly if our bodies are fat, scarred, or in some other way 'abnormal'), this is an overwhelmingly powerful

---

[61] Ibid.

message."[62] As a pushback against the wafer-thin, arrow-cheeked ideals espoused in large sections of American culture over the past few decades, the Body Positivity movement has done some good work, particularly in affecting who gets to represent brands in ads and on billboards.

We've seen Dove's #MyBeautyMySay campaign. This is an ad strategy that features a group of diverse women featuring different sizes, body shapes, and backgrounds. We've witnessed plus-size celebrities like *This Is Us* star Chrissy Metz light up the screen. Women are sharing unedited photos of their stretch marks and Rubenesque figures on social media. They're offering an unvarnished look at what pregnancy, surgery, illness, or just life itself naturally does to the body—inviting us to relate, to bear witness, and to shed shame. While things aren't perfect, at least they're better. Right?

Despite the Body Positivity movement having seemingly gone mainstream, studies have found that there are still major issues:

- Around 50% of thirteen-year-old girls report being unhappy with their bodies; this number leaps to 80% by the time girls hit seventeen.
- Nearly 80% of young teenage girls report fears of becoming fat.
- 60% of adult women think they are too heavy and are

---

[62] Stephanie Yeboah. "Why the Body Positivity Movement Still Has a Long Way to Go." *Vogue*, 29 May 2020. https://www.vogue.in/wellness/content/body-positivity-fat-acceptance-movement-still-has-a-long-way-to-go (Accessed March 8, 2021).

self-conscious about their weight.

- 30% of all women report being too uncomfortable in a swimsuit.[63]

While I'm all for a more diverse representation on signs and screens, the way we think about our bodies is informed by far more than just what we see. It's also informed by how we hear the people around us talk about their own bodies and the bodies of others.

Fat Acceptance

According to the National Association to Advance Fat Acceptance, advocating for fat acceptance is about "building a society in which people of every size are accepted with dignity and equality in all aspects of life" by seeking to "eliminate discrimination based on body size and provide fat people with the tools for self-empowerment through public education, advocacy and support."[64] Though Fat Acceptance has garnered less airtime in some circles than the Body Positivity movement, it is nevertheless an important component in the ongoing conversations surrounding weight, dignity, and personhood.

While some people fear that the Fat Acceptance movement will contribute to a rise in illnesses such as Type 2 diabetes and high blood pressure, "overweight people are pushing back against caregivers who they say fat-shame them and blame common

---

[63] Dr. Jake Linardon. "The Ultimate List of Body Image Statistics in 2021." *Break Binge Eating. https://breakbingeeating.com/body-image-statistics/* (Accessed March 9, 2021).

[64] "About Us." NAAFA. https://naafa.org/aboutus (Accessed March 11, 2021).

medical problems on their weight. Obesity, they say, isn't always the cause of their issues, and diet and exercise aren't always the solution."[65]

Whatever you may think about media manipulation of our body image, the pushback movements birthed, and the state of our body perceptions in general, please be careful how you talk about it. Christ-followers are in a wonderful position to gently and effectively enter this conversation. But they're also in the position to do plenty of harm. Some already have.

Thunder Thighs and Trophy Wives

When it comes to messages about our bodies, it would be unfair to blame the entire problem on the media—that is, on advertisers, movies, television, and the like. In many cases, the attacks on our bodies originate a bit closer to home—from those who refer to the shape of others' bodies with terms like "saddlebags" and "thunder thighs." Our co-workers. Our friends and family members. Our mentors and our peers. Even our spiritual authorities themselves.

In February of 2021, a pastor at a church in the Midwest used part of his sermon to publicly attack the appearance of women who, in his opinion, "let themselves go" after marriage. He then preached weight control as a solution to marital problems.

---

[65] Joseph P. Williams. "The Great Body-Acceptance Debate." *U.S. News.* https://www.usnews.com/news/healthiest-communities/articles/2020-02-03/body-positivity-weight-bias-and-the-battle-for-a-healthy-life (Accessed May 6, 2021).

"Don't give him a reason to be looking around," he admonishes women regarding their husbands, implying that physical appearance is the root cause of infidelity. While standing in front of the congregation with an open Bible in hand, this pastor then says, "Now look, I'm not saying every woman can be the epic, the epic trophy wife of all time like Melania Trump."

At this point, a picture of the former First Lady wearing a low-cut, light blue gown appears behind him on the jumbo screen.

"All I can say is not everybody looks like that, amen? . . . But you don't need to look like a butch either."[66]

There are many troubling aspects to this sermon, not the least of which is that the trophy wife status—in which a woman's main attraction is her appearance—is held up by someone in a position of spiritual authority as something women should aspire to. This pastor completely disregards the Scriptural wisdom that charm is deceitful and beauty fleeting, and that it's a woman's fear of the Lord as seen in her godly conduct that is to be praised—not how her body looks in a strapless ball gown.[67]

It might be easy to consider this man an outlier and chalk the resulting online uproar as a tempest in a teapot; however, the truth is, the pastor didn't make these comments in a vacuum. He made these comments to an audience, in front of God and everybody. In fact, he'd preached sermons like these in the past, with no evidence

---

[66] Adelle M. Banks. "After sermon criticizing wives' weight, pastor resigns as moderator of General Baptist meeting." *Religion News Service.* https://religionnews.com/2021/03/02/after-sermon-criticizing-wives-weight-pastor-resigns-as-moderator-of-general-baptist-meeting/ (Accessed March 15, 2021).
[67] Proverbs 31.

of resulting church discipline.[68] Has anyone from his inner circle or congregation challenged him on these matters? Pressed in on some awkward conversations? Perhaps. I don't presume to know everyone he knows, or the full nuance of his relationships within his church. All we have to go on is the video that was released publicly, and it's clear from the sounds the congregation is making that while there may certainly have been those who were shocked by his statements, there are plenty who were both approving and appreciative of such talk.

As I listened to the clip, my heart went out to those who live in the homes, sit around the dinner tables, and listen to the conversations of such people. Have friends of mine received marriage counseling from a pastor who believes and teaches such things? What's the small-group and family culture like in such congregations? How do our sisters and brothers who do not match the idealized body standard fare emotionally, psychologically, and spiritually in such environments? Where do these precious souls turn for a sympathetic and listening ear?

Let's Talk

People discussing weight, shapes, and body images in negative ways have caused much harm. But the answer to this

---

[68] Hemant Mehta. "After Baptist Pastor Tells Wives to Lose Weight, His Church is in Crisis Mode." *Patheos: The Friendly Atheist.* https://friendlyatheist.patheos.com/2021/03/02/after-baptist-pastor-tells-wives-to-lose-weight-his-church-is-in-crisis-mode/?utm_source=dlvr.it&utm_medium=twitter (Accessed March 15, 2021).

problem is not to over-correct and never talk about these things. What matters is how we talk about our bodies and why.

And make no mistake: we need to talk more about our bodies and how they relate to our spiritual formation. As we will investigate further in Chapter 9, these discussions must address more than simply weight and shape but must be broadened to include physical pain, chronic conditions, and disabilities as well. While we can do harm in the way we talk about these things, we can also do harm in never addressing them at all.

Many Christians believe that we can be good, faithful followers without properly addressing the needs and issues related to our bodies. That as people who look forward to a better kingdom, we should not dwell too much on temporary things below but should keep our minds on "higher things." While I think there's a place for this sort of application, the idea that we should abandon our connections to the physical world in favor of some purely spiritual, theoretical reality carries a strong flavor of Gnosticism.

Gnosticism is an ages-old framework that focuses exclusively on the inner, spiritual life to the detriment of physical flourishing. Though the term *Christian Gnosticism* is somewhat of an oxymoron, since the tenets of Gnosticism aren't in line with Christian teachings, there have certainly been times throughout church history during which Gnostic principles have influenced how believers thought and behaved. While it's difficult to condense Gnostic teaching into a summary small enough for our purpose, Gnosticism basically boils down to a foundational belief that the physical world is bad and wrong, while the spiritual realm is good and right.

Obviously, this contradicts God's own view of his physical creation—which he viewed as "very good." At any rate, this sort of strictly dichotomous thinking has led to outright heresies (such as Docetism, which taught that Jesus only appeared to have a man's body) as well as twisted, damaging spiritual practices (such as Medieval Christians literally beating their bodies and living bleak and austere lives, having deemed the simple pleasures of life bad).

Failing to address issues related to weight, health, and body image could stem from practical Gnosticism, but it could also arise from a very natural fear of saying the wrong thing. And indeed, we must be cautious about how we address these issues.

As we've seen, how we talk about our bodies can prove harmful. While the Bible does have things to say about gluttony and how we should care for our bodies as temples of the Holy Spirit, Scripture doesn't classify these issues according to body type or shape. Gluttony is about much more than simply eating too much—it's about unregulated desires. Not all large people are gluttons, and not all small people are free of this sin. This is why in calling us to himself, God addresses the deeper, more rooted issues rather than the sizes and shapes and relative health of our bodies. In and of themselves, these proofs can be deceiving.

In writing on these matters, author Amanda Martinez Beck says, "The message that the kingdom of God is best demonstrated by healthy people, unintentional as it may be, is contrary to the gospel and damaging to people created in the image of God. The danger of this message is that people who don't meet the subliminal or overt physical standards will discount what they have to offer to their brothers and sisters in the Church. They will feel like second-class citizens in the kingdom, but the truth is that everybody can love and serve God."[69]

What We Lose

Who decides which bodies have value? Who decides who has the ideal weight, shape, skin tone, vibe, and look? Why do we even have concepts of idealized sizes, shapes, and appearances? There are deep issues in play here, ones we will never get to the bottom of if we don't allow our orthodoxy to shape our conversations around these matters. When we allow the cultural narrative to control this conversation, the answers will vary depending on ever-fluctuating changes to who has enough cultural power to control the message.

I won't lie to you: discussing issues relating to weight and personal appearance will always be awkward. This isn't just an issue for women, either. Although cultural beauty standards for women are high, men and boys who do not fit the idealized format of the All-American athletic male often feel inadequate as well. However difficult this discussion may be, there are reasons why it's worth it to press through the discomfort to engage these topics.

First, when we fail to engage these topics empathetically, we cede authority to the loudest voices in the room—whether those be

---

[69] Amanda Martinez Beck. "Oprah's Best Body and the Body of Christ." *Christ and Pop Culture.* *https://christandpopculture.com/oprahs-best-body-and-the-body-of-christ/* (Accessed August 6, 2021).

voices worth listening to or not. Second, if we consistently fail to show ourselves open to honest dialogue around issues of weight and body image, we remain closed to the holistic experience of our sisters and brothers in Christ.

If the only time others hear us mention someone's appearance is to comment on their relative attractiveness, we could be unwittingly communicating something about ourselves and an unconscious value we place on outward forms and features. Or, like the rest of us, you could just be worried about saying the wrong thing, hurting someone's feelings, and scarring them for life with hurtful words.

But what if there's something in the middle? What if there's a way to talk about weight, size, body shape, and our personal appearance that is helpful and constructive? What if there's a way to address it which is deeply formative, particularly for our children, who hear and absorb everything? Such conversations could flow in many directions, but they all find their source in the same deep well.

Whose Image

One of my favorite things about reading the gospels is the dialogue between Jesus and his followers. It's clear that many who approached him did so with an agenda, and yet even with their forward planning, talks with Jesus just never seemed to go as they hoped.

I especially love how Jesus handles combative, bad-faith questions and questioners. Not only were they never able to trip him up, but they always walked away with a much deeper convictional question ringing in their ears.

This is exactly what we see recorded in Mark 12. The Pharisees approached Jesus with an intent to entrap him with a question about taxes. We know this is a trap because the Scriptures state this intention directly. But the question also originates from the Pharisees and the Herodians, two groups that normally wouldn't have anything to do with each other. Yet here they are, teaming up to take Jesus down.

They ask Jesus whether it's right to pay imperial taxes to Caesar. But instead of making this question one of mere political intrigue, Jesus uses it as an opportunity. He broadens the scope of the question, deepening its implications.[70]

After they ask their tricky question, he asks for them to bring him a denarius, a type of common silver coin that had been in circulation for several hundred years by that point. At the time, it was equivalent to a day's wage.

> They brought the coin, and he asked them, "Whose image is this? And whose inscription?"
> "Caesar's," they replied.
> Then Jesus said to them, "Give back to Caesar what is Caesar's and to God what is God's."[71]

While this is a passage of Scripture I have heard quoted in

---

[70] Victor Babajide Cole, "Mark" in *Africa Bible Commentary*, ed. Tokunboh Adeyemo (Grand Rapids: Zondervan, 2006), 1218.
[71] Mark 12:16-17.

sermons from the time of my youth, I most often heard it referenced in defense of Christians paying taxes. But, as Jen Wilkin writes, this story is not actually about taxes at all. The denarius Jesus held up would have been minted with the face and inscription of Emperor Tiberius, whose father Augustus had been worshipped as a god during his lifetime. In talking about the inscription on the coin, Jesus is taking a question about taxes and turning it into a point about image-bearing.

> He says, in effect, "The coin is engraved with the image of a god, marking what belongs to him. You, on the other hand, are engraved with the image of God himself, marking what belongs to him. Will you concern yourself with earthly obligations to the neglect of the heavenly ones required by the image engraved in you? "You bear the very marks of the Creator. Render unto God what is God's."[72]

It is from this passage that Christians gain important language for how we speak about our fellow human beings. They also are image-bearers of God. As such, they are worthy of respect, dignity, and honor by virtue of the image stamped on them. How we talk about fellow image-bearers—how we treat them, engage with them, and honor them—is a reflection of the respect we have not just for them but for the one whose image they bear.

---

[72] Jen Wilkin. *In His Image: 10 Ways God Calls Us to Reflect His Character*. (Wheaton: Crossway, 2018), 150.

All our conversations surrounding weight, physical appearance, and body issues have to center on this one foundational concept. This concept undergirds how we think about—and therefore talk about—one another. We cannot view our fellow human beings as bearers of the image of an ineffable God and then talk about them in ways that are harsh, hateful, or cruel. We cannot mock and disparage them. To disrespect that image is to disrespect him.

Start Your Own Awkward Conversation

Find some trusted conversation partners for discussion or consider the questions on your own.

1. As a general rule, in what situations do you tend to talk about weight, appearance, and body image? Are your comments—whether directed at yourself or others—generally positive or negative?

2. In your opinion, who should be leading discussions about these issues? Where can we turn to find valuable messages about our health and our bodies?

3. Can you think of a time when talking about issues surrounding body image have been helpful to you? Harmful? How have these conversations affected you long-term?

4. Discuss the forces that have shaped your view of your own body. How could people of faith combat the damage being done?

5. What could we gain by pressing through discomfort to engage socially awkward conversations regarding weight and body image?

Welcome to Awkwardsville:
Awkward in Auckland

In 2015, I was in New Zealand, with my sister Bethany. We had reached the tail end of a successful trip, having already spent time down in Wellington and hiking Tongariro Alpine Crossing in North Island's National Park.

On this day, we'd spent the day in downtown Auckland, nipping in and out of the shops, treating ourselves to a lavish brunch slathered in New Zealand butter, and enjoying the low-key city vibe unique to this part of the world.

Toward the end of the day, as we started to make our way back to our host's house for the night, we found ourselves at a busy traffic crossing. I stood next to Bethany talking to her about something deep. Mid-soliloquy, I turned my head the opposite direction to look down the street. A brief pause stretched between us, during which I gathered my thoughts. I turned back around to deliver the last sentence of my monologue,

"There's just so much to think about," I said, my eyes round and my voice intense, directly into the face of the person standing on my right—who was no longer Bethany.

The young guy next to me startled. His eyebrows went up and he stepped back.

So did I.

Surely, I could explain this to him. But he didn't seem interested. In fact, he inched sideways, putting space between us.

The light changed, and we scuttled across the street behind him as he quick-walked away. I whisper-hissed the story to Bethany as we walked up to our bus stop, and true to the way that my life works, there he was, sitting under the sign. Not only that, we wound up taking the same bus.

"It's okay," Bethany told me when I paid my fare and sidled down the aisle, observing my unintentional conversation partner studiously avoiding eye contact. "On a Ruth Scale, this actually wasn't so bad."

CHAPTER 6
Call Me Crazy

When I was sixteen, one of our neighbors took issue with her sons having water fights. They would turn on the outside faucets for long periods of time, muddying the lawn and wasting gallons of water. Her solution? She hacksawed the spigots off the side of the house. No more water fights.

Simple and brilliant—if a bit extreme. But this is how things tended to go for this family. The mother of the house would wake up one morning and decide she'd had enough, and the next thing we knew, the spigots were gone. Or she would host an impromptu yard sale to sell every item her children had failed to put away after she'd told them to—many of which were items they'd borrowed from the rest of the neighborhood. I had to buy back my own Nintendo *Marble Madness* cartridge. I don't remember even trying to convince her it was mine. I think by that point, I knew that to deal with her was to do so on her terms.

The adults in our social circles marveled over her behavior—occasionally worrying and sometimes snickering about some of her more outlandish shenanigans. But I don't remember anyone ever expressing a hint of what is so clear to me now: that this woman lived with some sort of mental or emotional illness. Growing up in the 80s and 90s, however, we didn't hear much about mental and emotional health or the benefits of medications and therapy.

If anyone we knew was in therapy, I had never been told. Mental health issues, even ones so overt that they absolutely must be acknowledged, were stigmatized. Things have changed over the decades, of course, and much of the change has been for the better. Now we see people openly discussing their mental health practices, walking around in hoodies reading *Jesus & Therapy*. Even pets have psychologists.

What's changed in the conversations surrounding mental health over the years? Could talking about mental health issues more often actually bring increased clarity?

Mixed Feelings

When it comes to disclosing mental health issues, many people experience mixed emotions. While support from friends, family members, and loved ones can be a key factor in managing mental health, disclosing a mental illness can lead to stigma. That is why some people don't disclose their challenges to others or seek treatment in the first place. It is estimated that 70% of people with mental illnesses receive no care from trained healthcare staff. While there are a variety of reasons why people might not seek care—including a lack of awareness and lack of access—two of the top four factors include prejudice and an expectation of discrimination against people diagnosed with a mental illness.[73]

How Did We Get Here?

I can't tell you how many times I've put off visiting a doctor, even in situations when it was clear I wasn't going to get better without help. Even with funds and access to care, there always seems to be a natural resistance. Most recently, I broke out in an astounding case of hives that steadily worsened by the hour, and yet I put the visit off for days and days, losing sleep and letting my skin crack open in an effort to postpone what amounted to a twenty-minute visit.

As much as you might chuckle over the relatability of that anecdote—because, seriously, who *does* like going to the doctor?—there is an even greater barrier to seeking mental health care than there is physical health care.[74]

Of course, this mental health versus physical health dichotomy is somewhat of a misnomer in itself. The brain is a part of the body, and the emotions are often inextricably linked to our physical state. Yet mental health/physical health is the language we're currently using to discuss matters of our total personhood.

My point here isn't to argue semantics but to ask perhaps a more important question: How did we get here, to the place where

---

[73] Henderson, C., Evans-Lacko, S., & Thornicroft, G. (2013). Mental illness stigma, help seeking, and public health programs. *American journal of public health*, *103*(5), 777–780. https://doi.org/10.2105/AJPH.2012.301056 (Accessed March 25, 2021).
[74] Ibid.

people in need of mental health services do not seek the very help they need? Could it be that the ways in which we've discussed mental illness in the past have contributed to an atmosphere of prejudice and discrimination? And could it be that some of us have done harm by failing to talk about mental illness at all?

The Butt of the Joke

In the early 2000s, pop star Britney Spears experienced a public mental health crisis. If you lived in the United States around this time, you couldn't have missed the shocking tabloid photos depicting her shaving her head, round-eyed and stressed out, and attacking a paparazzi's SUV with an umbrella. I had never been one to keep up with pop culture, particularly in those years. But even I knew something was up with Britney Spears. This woman was distressed—breaking down and crying in public. She was clearly in shambles. How did the nation respond? By and large, they mocked her. Back in the early 2000s, everyone from daytime talk show hosts to late-night comedians to media legends like Diane Sawyer had something to say about the young and struggling pop star, turning her into an object of ridicule and the butt of jokes.

One person who refused to be swept up in the tide of disdain was Scottish comedian Craig Ferguson. As the host of *The Late Late Show with Craig Ferguson*, he delivered an opening monologue on Presidents' Day in 2007 that went against the tide. He was certain it was going to get him fired. And no wonder. Not only did he refuse to mock Spears, but he called out others in the media for doing so—and his own audience for laughing at the jokes.

The way the audience responds is telling. If you ever listen to the clip, you will notice that from the instant Ferguson says Spears's name, the audience is primed to laugh. He hasn't made any jokes about her—he's simply mentioned her name—and yet there are already cackles. Perhaps this reaction can be attributed in part to the nature of the environment. When you're in the presence of a comedian, you are primed to laugh. But I think there's something else going on here, and Ferguson seemed to think so, too.

Ferguson started by acknowledging Presidents' Day and using this as a segue to express how thankful he is for the freedom of speech. He then announced his intention to talk about something "a little bit different tonight." He mentioned having met Kevin Costner at an event after having made fun of him on air. Costner was polite but seemed uncomfortable, and it made Ferguson wonder, "At what price am I doing this stuff?"

When he asks this question, the audience laughs. Perhaps all this introspection has been set-up for a joke, or perhaps they're feeling uncomfortable and not sure how to express it. But Ferguson is not done with his *mea culpa*. His comedic aim has been off, he says, and it's hurting people. He laments that amid all the jokes, "people are dying" and mentions that Anna Nicole Smith had recently died. The audience laughs again, this time more loudly.

"It's not a *joke*," he tells them earnestly. Seeming to finally sense his sincerity, the audience quiets a bit; but when he tells them he's not going to be telling any Britney Spears jokes that night, they laugh again. They can't seem to catch on that he's trying to be straight with them.

Ferguson continues, pushing forward with his plea despite their obviously dissonant reaction.

> Tonight, no Britney Spears jokes, and here's why... I'm not doing them... The kind of weekend she had—she was checking in and out of rehab, she was shaving her head, getting tattoos—that's what she was doing this weekend. This Sunday, I was fifteen years sober. So, I looked at her weekend, and I looked at my own weekend, and I thought, "You know, I'd rather have my weekend." But what she's going through reminds me of what I was doing. It's an anniversary, you start to think about it, and it reminds me of where I was fifteen years ago, when I was living like that... This woman has two kids. She's twenty-five years old. She's a baby herself. She's a baby, you know. And the thing is, you can embarrass somebody to death.[75]

Whether because of his own personal experience or some other insight, Craig Ferguson got it in a way other people around

---

[75] Elizabeth Logan. "This 2007 Video of Craig Ferguson Refusing to Make Fun of Britney Spears Is Going Viral." *Glamour.* *https://www.glamour.com/story/this-2007-video-of-craig-ferguson-refusing-to-make-fun-of-britney-spears-is-going-viral* (Accessed March 26, 2021)

the same time were failing to get it. Britney Spears didn't need mockery. She needed help. And although most of us at the time weren't in a position to help her directly, our attitude towards her and others like her said a lot to those around us about our underlying attitudes toward mental illness. And those messages were not good.

What We're Saying and Not Saying

In my observations, there are two layers keeping us from having productive discussions surrounding mental health. While one of those layers is certainly avoidance, the other is an insidious and destructive misuse of mental health language.

Avoidance

Because I grew up in very conservative church circles, my first assumption regarding why I haven't heard much productive dialogue about mental health was that those around me did not believe in the validity of mental health diagnoses or the importance of trained, professional mental health care.

To my relief, when I set out to prove this theory, it quickly crumbled. I talked with two pastors from my past. Both of them affirmed the reality and necessity of mental health care and openly discussed examples of situations in which they would counsel someone from the Bible or refer them for professional care and treatment. This anecdotal evidence lined up with what I found in the numbers.

Writing for *Christianity Today,* Ed Stetzer says this:

When we surveyed Protestant pastors, the first thing we discovered is that they do, in fact, have experience with mental illnesses. Approximately three out of four pastors said they knew at least one family member, friend or congregant who had been diagnosed with bipolar disorder.

Close to the same number (74%) said they knew someone diagnosed with clinical depression. More than half (57%) said they knew at least three people who fell into that category. In terms of counseling, almost six in 10 (59%) said they had counseled at least one person who was eventually diagnosed with an acute mental illness.

Perhaps even more important, 23% of pastors indicated they had battled a mental illness of some kind on a personal level, including 12% who said it was formally diagnosed. These findings are confirmed by the National Alliance on Mental Illness and similar numbers within the general population.[76]

On the surface, all of this is very encouraging. Pastors experience mental illnesses at the same rate as those of us in the general population, and for those of us involved in Protestant

---

[76] Ed Stetzer. "The Church and Mental Health: What Do the Numbers Tell Us?" *Christianity Today.* https://www.christianitytoday.com/edstetzer/2018/april/church-and-mental-health.html (Accessed March 26, 2021).

churches in America, we can largely rest assured that our spiritual leaders have an awareness of these issues and know enough to acknowledge that they're important and should be taken seriously.

Yet despite statistical evidence that one in five American adults experiences a mental health issue,[77] research shows that 65% of pastors speak to their churches in sermons or large group messages about mental illness once a year, rarely, or never . . . and another 26% only speak about it several times a year.

Lamenting this gap, Ed Stetzer reminds us that "Sermons break stigmas. When pastors are willing to talk publicly about mental illness, they take away some of the shame associated with these conditions. Churches need to be much more willing to acknowledge and destigmatize the presence of mental health issues in their faith communities."[78]

What's true from the pulpit is true on an interpersonal level. When we act as if depression, therapy, counseling, trauma, bi-polar, anxiety, and a host of mental health issues do not exist, we do not foster an environment in which those who are mentally ill can be open and honest with us about what they're dealing with.

If that "one in five" statistic sounded disproportionate to you based on your personal experience, that doesn't necessarily mean you don't know people living with a mental health diagnosis. It

---

[77] Jeremy Smith. "Mental Health Statistics" *Church and Mental Health.* https://churchandmentalhealth.com/mental-health-statistics/ (Accessed March 28, 2021).

[78] Ed Stetzer. "Necessary Conversations: The Church, Suicide, and Mental Health." *Christianity Today.* *https://www.christianitytoday.com/edstetzer/2018/august/necessary-conversations-church-suicide-and-mental-health.html* (Accessed March 28, 2021).

simply could mean you don't know that you know those people. At this point, it could be worth taking the time to ask yourself why that is.

Misuse

When we're not avoiding talking about mental health issues, we're often guilty of misusing the terms to make disparaging comments about others and sometimes even ourselves. Like most who have watched the NBC sitcom *Parks and Rec,* I have a soft spot for the lovable-but-irascible character Tom Haverford, portrayed by Aziz Ansari. This flippant and flighty wannabe playboy possesses a level of self-confidence bordering on farcical, especially considering his serial failures in business and romance. Early in Season 3, as he discusses one of his recent romantic entanglements, Tom says this about his ex-girlfriend Lucy: "She broke up with me. Didn't really tell me why. Luckily, when you're the guy, you can just tell people she's crazy."[79]

We laugh because it's Tom—but also because it's true.

Witness the "crazy ex-girlfriend" phenomenon, a convenient trope that men have historically employed to absolve themselves of guilt and prop up their egos when exiting a relationship. Not only can this be a form of gaslighting, in which women's strong emotions are not acknowledged as valid, but it can also serve as cover for what men may actually mean: "She was upset, and I

---

[79] *Parks and Recreation*, "Time Capsule," directed by Michael Schur (NBC, 2011)

didn't want her to be."[80]

Misusing mental health terms to serve our own purposes is not limited to men, of course.

- "The weather is so bi-polar today."
- "These rules are so psychotic."
- "I'm sorry, I'm a little OCD about this."

When we use words this way, we lessen the impact of their legitimate use and treat these diagnoses as a punchline rather than the serious and life-altering conditions that they are. As anyone with clinical OCD will tell you, there's no such thing as being "a little" OCD.

Obsessive Compulsive Disorder is a serious mental illness that causes repeated, unwanted thoughts or sensations that turn into obsessions and compel someone to repeat actions over and over again. These compulsions can consume hours of each day, feel beyond the control of the person carrying them out, are not enjoyable, and strongly interfere with work, social interactions, and personal lives.[81] Liking your books stacked neatly or your

---

[80] Harris O'Malley. "Men Really Need to Stop Calling Women Crazy." *The Washington Post.*
https://www.washingtonpost.com/posteverything/wp/2014/07/09/men-really-need-to-stop-calling-women-crazy/
(Accessed March 28, 2021).
[81] "Obsessive-Compulsive Disorder (OCD)" *WebMD*, reviewed by Smitha Bhandari, MD. https://www.webmd.com/mental-health/obsessive-compulsive-disorder#:~:text=Obsessive%2Dcompulsive%20disorder%20(OCD)%20is%20a%20mental%20illness%20that,nails%20or%20thinking%20negative%20thoughts (Accessed March 28, 2021).

closet organized doesn't make you "a little OCD." It just makes you person who values order and tidiness.

"People sometimes use terms that are meant to describe a mental illness to exaggerate a slightly stressful situation, to make a joke online or to insult another person," writes Katie Fusillo in an opinion piece for *Arizona State University's* student-run news site *The State Press.* "However, this practice is incredibly harmful. Falsely labeling mental illnesses . . . waters down these words so that people who deal with mental illnesses no longer have the language to accurately express their experiences" in a way that will be taken seriously by others.[82]

Suppose one of your family members died by suicide. Then suppose a frustrated friend or neighbor, while blowing off steam, said something like, "I just can take it anymore. If this doesn't stop soon, I'm going to blow my brains out." Let's say this was a common way people talked around you. How might you know who was being serious and who was being hyperbolic?

Talking It Out

Our sisters and brothers with mental health challenges have articulated that they don't share about their conditions more often because they are afraid of facing backlash and stigma. And no wonder, given that many of us grew up only hearing about mental health diagnoses when they were framed as jokes.

---

[82] Katie Fusillo. "Opinion: Mental illness shouldn't be the butt of the joke." https://www.statepress.com/article/2018/09/spopinion-dont-use-mental-health-terms-casually (Accessed March 28, 2021).

How can we help create an open and welcoming environment in which we can come together and talk it out? When Ed Stetzer mentioned pastors being pivotal in this, I believe he was onto something. Because faith and community leaders are often the first point of contact when individuals and families face mental health crises and traumatic events,[83] real change could be possible if more pastors and leaders took initiative in these areas:

- Identifying practical ways to support people with mental health issues or illnesses.
- Connecting individuals and families to help.
- Educating communities and congregations.
- Promoting acceptance of those with mental illnesses.[84]

Perhaps you don't consider yourself a leader. Does this let you off the hook? Each of us can become leaders in our circles of influence and initiate change in conversations around mental illnesses and mental health. For each of us, this may look a bit different.

- Being open about our own mental health.
- Encouraging treatment, counseling, therapy, etc.
- Praising those making strides and encouraging those who need it.

---

[83] "For Community and Faith Leaders." MentalHealth.gov. https://www.mentalhealth.gov/talk/faith-community-leaders (Accessed March 29, 2021).
[84] Ibid.

- Providing nurturing conversational spaces for others to open up about their challenges, struggles, triumphs, and the need for ongoing work.

Will such conversations be awkward? Almost certainly—especially at first. Should the fear of potential awkwardness stop us? I don't believe so, especially considering the high risks of continuing in silence versus the high rewards available for those of us willing to speak out.

In the context of a long, heart-felt conversation, I asked a friend who has been dealing with a lifelong emotional battle if she had considered getting therapy. I don't think it's what she expected me to say, but once those beats of awkward silence passed, we were able to engage in a fruitful discussion weighing the merits of both pastoral counseling and therapy. It was awkward at first, but in the end, it was good.

Everything to Gain

What do we lose by failing to engage in important conversations surrounding issues of mental health with our family members, friends, and loved ones? If the statistics prove true in our own circles, that would mean we'd be failing to engage holistically with the experience of 20% of the people in our lives. We miss the opportunity to cheer, encourage, come alongside, and support those among us who perhaps need love and understanding more than most. And this is a serious matter: "46% of people who die by suicide had a known mental health condition."[85]

As for what we could gain by pressing through discomfort to engage socially awkward conversations regarding mental health, the primary reward is self-evident. Normalizing open discussion on matters of mental health creates an environment in which more people can express their needs and get help. Those under care can live authentically without fear of stigma. And those who co-exist with mental health diagnoses can openly share the tools, skills, and helps that have proven effective in their situations. In God's plan, we need each other in every area of our lives—including mental health.

Start Your Own Awkward Conversation

Find some trusted conversation partners for discussion or consider the questions on your own.

1. Name the barriers that keep people from being open about their mental health.

2. How has your environmental upbringing influenced your views on mental illness and things like therapy and medications?

3. In what ways can we foster openness and trusting

---

[85] National Alliance on Mental Illness (NAMI), "Risk of Suicide," https://www.nami.org/About-Mental-Illness/Common-with-Mental-Illness/Risk-of-Suicide (Accessed June 7, 2021).

environments in which people can feel comfortable sharing about their mental health needs?

4. Discuss the role of pastors, spiritual leaders, and community leaders in destigmatizing mental health issues.

Welcome to Awkwardsville:

Whispering Hope

For a time, I somehow morphed into my church's unofficial funeral musician. My musical strengths are more vocal than anything else, but my parents insisted that each of us kids study either piano or organ when we were growing up. Despite rarely ever playing anymore, I've retained just enough skill at the keyboard to struggle through a song or two when absolutely necessary. By "absolutely necessary," I mean everyone else who could possibly play has already said no, and organizers are now scraping the bottom of the barrel.

Usually, I would prefer to say no as well. I'm not exaggerating when I tell you that playing the piano at an event will require part-time-job levels of practice to prepare, and I will likely still play like a clockwork musical monkey, only I'll be mashing my hands against the keys instead of clanging a set of cymbals. But when it comes to funerals, I simply can't say no.

On one such occasion, I was required to learn a new piece. Well, I don't know that I can call it "new." It was written in 1868. But it was new to me. "Whispering Hope" is a 19th century hymn, and it shows. The melody soars and dips, alternating high and low in swoopy swings. You really have to keep your wits about you, because those sudden octave jumps are not for the faint of heart.

I would have preferred an extra week to practice, but funerals run on their own timelines. Between the moment I was asked to play for the service and the event itself, I only had three days to prepare. I showed up clad in black, sweating profusely from the armpits.

The song leader and I met a few minutes early to run through the songs together. If anything, this only further heightened my unease. My fingers tangled, and I bobbled the transitions. He asked if we should run through them again, and I said I didn't think it would help.

As soon as the song leader stepped to the podium and lifted his hands to cue the intro, something came over me. A cozy blanket of fatalism settled reassuringly on my shoulders. Whatever happened, it was now too late to do anything to change it. I lifted my hands, flexed them over the keys, and played in a way I never had in practice. We sailed through the song, notes rising and falling in just the right places, mourners singing along in harmony.

When the service ended, I darted for the ladies' room. This wasn't to avoid talking to any of the family members or mourners: the eulogizing had run long, and I felt a genuinely pressing need. I'd made it to the back hallway, bathroom in sight, when an elderly gentleman, as if lying in wait, side-stepped directly into my path. His face was warm and open, his hands folded gently over the handle a wooden cane.

"Ah, excuse me," I said, trying to side-step.

He shuffled as well. "I have a question, miss."

"Okay." I gazed over his shoulder. The bathroom was so close.

"If I promised to buy you a piano and asked you to marry me, would you say yes and play for me every night?"

Reader, I turned him down. Quickly, as matters were pressing.

But it's nice to know I can still attract suitors—even while standing in front of a bathroom at a funeral.

CHAPTER 7
No Middle Ground

The year 2020 caused huge political waves on both sides of the aisle. Christians found themselves not only taking sides but enduring battles and relational strain regardless of the position they took.

The circumstances of the day didn't help. A particularly contentious election was on the line with the parties and the media nipping, growling, and biting at one another. Our country, along with the entire world, was drowning in a lethal virus that shut down life as we knew it. Open arguments surrounding all aspects of this virus raged on, along with all the conspiracy theories that went with them.

After viewing one particular news story, I found myself posting my opinions on Facebook. This isn't a move I would normally have made, but the circumstance of the moment was so drastic that I felt I had to speak out. I shared about what I thought was an absolute wrong, both politically and morally. I then declared my intention not to "squabble" with anyone in the comments—a declaration I eventually thought better of and apologized for. Not only was the word *squabble* needlessly provocative, but I was going against my own ethos by shutting down potentially productive dialogue rather than encouraging it. In the end, I did engage with the comments, and I can't say it went well or proved satisfying for any of us involved.

By that point, I had already seen evidence of the pattern Christian historian Kristin Kobes Du Mez describes in her book *Jesus and John Wayne:* that while American evangelicals self-identify as "Bible-believing Christians," a portion of them actually cling not to the faith itself but to "a broader set of deeply held values communicated through symbol, ritual, and political allegiances."[86] While it wouldn't be fair to lump every American Christian into this, if we know how to look, we'll see ample evidence. In this polarized political climate, even people of faith can define themselves more in terms of what they're against than what they're for.

What You're Against or What You're For

In the 2015 smash hit musical *Hamilton*, Lin Manuel Miranda depicts Aaron Burr as advising the then-inexperienced Alexander Hamilton at the beginning of his political career. Burr tells Hamilton to talk less and smile more, never letting anyone know what he's against or what he's for. [87] The subtext here is that

---

[86] Kristin Kobes Du Mez. *Jesus and John Wayne: How White Evangelicals Corrupted a Faith and Fractured a Nation.* (New York: Liverlight Publishing Corporation, 2020), 297.

[87] Miranda, Lin-Manuel. "Hamilton: An American Musical." In *Hamilton: The Revolution.* Edited by Jeremy McCarter. New York: Grand Central Publishing, 2016.

Hamilton would get ahead politically by not running his mouth and offending people. It's advice I've never been able to follow.

Neither can Hamilton, as it happens. But that's another story.

What gets me into trouble within my own community is not when I call out the sins and evils of society—bringing Scripture to bear on the moral lapses we see from the world. Or even necessarily, when I turn those same indictments inward and point them toward evils within the bounds of the church. What gets me into trouble is when following Scripture faithfully leads me to differing conclusions on political and social concerns. When I violate the unspoken values of symbol, ritual, and political allegiance du Mez described in her book.

As a result of experiencing painful fallout after some of these conversations, I've come to see just how difficult it is to hold these discussions without getting sucked into immediate defensiveness. It's so easy to feel ganged up on when I hold a minority opinion. That feeling in itself can morph into an emotion-driven tirade that has less to do with my beliefs and more to do with my frustration at the injustice of the treatment I'm experiencing.

Before we can engage in profitable discussions around politics, we need to ask ourselves a deeper foundational question: how can we openly and honestly discuss something this volatile with the same love and compassion with which we discuss every other topic in this book?

Our Basic Framework

Perhaps political discussions are so challenging because

we've forgotten that the basic Christian framework applies to them as it does to all other topics. All too often, we behave as if the spiritual part of life is over here, separate and distinct from other aspects of life, including politics. Perhaps, like me, you have heard other Christians emphasize that Jesus didn't come to build a political kingdom but a spiritual one.

While it's true that Jesus stated that his kingdom is not of this world, that doesn't mean we totally divorce our Christian faith and practice from political engagement. In reality, politics and everything else is totally swallowed up by our faith, a belief system that encompasses our entire lives. Every single attitude we hold and action we take should be patterned after the example of Jesus and his gospel.

Through his life and ministry, Jesus left us a pattern to follow. This pattern applies to every mode of life and could frankly have been included in any other chapter of this book. I include it here, however, because all too often we see examples of people who claim the name of Christ behaving nothing at all like Jesus—all in the name of politics. And that's a problem.

In his life and ministry, here's the basic pattern Jesus left for us:

- I will leave a place of comfort.
- I will come to you.
- I will lay aside power to serve you.
- I will do things for you that you cannot do for yourself.
- I am willing to suffer for your sake.

As Christians living in our current political systems, we can follow this pattern in order to bridge divides and point others toward timeless truths.

I Will Leave a Place of Comfort

Talking about politics is rarely comfortable. Which is why many of us prefer to leave the room when Uncle Randy starts spouting his off-the-wall political theories at the family reunion. But if no one pulls Uncle Randy aside or respectfully opens an awkward but necessary conversation, 1) Uncle Randy will assume he's right or 2) Uncle Randy will assume that everyone must agree with him or 3) Uncle Randy could miss access to key information he needs to change his mind or 4) young or otherwise impressionable listeners may assume there are no counterpoints to Uncle Randy's arguments.

I don't enjoy political debate, but I know I need to engage with it. I need to hear from people who hold different viewpoints, and they need to hear from me. If we exist only in echo chambers, we miss the richness of community. Remember, in God's plan we all need each other, and sometimes what people most need from us is a counterpoint—and that may require us to step out of our comfort zones.

What leaving your place of comfort will look like for you may differ from what it looks like for me. I've already admitted my tendency to morph into the "Well, Actually" Girl. For me, I've had to find balance between saying everything I know at all times and saying nothing. There are times when either of those options could be off base. In each conversation, I have to ask what it means to love God well and love my neighbor as myself in this moment. Sometimes that means speaking out. Sometimes that means staying quiet. Sometimes that means waiting to ask a wiser, calmer person how I should approach the issue. I will let you guess which of those options, for me, involves leaving my place of comfort. I can't say I strike the right note every time. But it's important that I'm trying.

I Will Come to You

In Jesus, we see what it looks like when a rescuer comes to us. As his followers, we must consider what it looks like to mirror this approach to others. This includes tackling tough topics. Rather than avoiding the problem, we go meet people where they are.

"I wish I heard more people talking about [fill in the blank]."

If you've ever found yourself thinking this about a specific political or social issue, perhaps it's time to pivot that thought to "I need to talk more about [fill in the blank]."

As we've already discussed, it doesn't matter whether you currently think of yourself as a leader. We listen to leaders because they are leading; and we become leaders by leading.

As leaders, we mirror the way of Jesus when we're willing to begin the discussions and actively participate in them rather than wishing someone else would bear that burden of responsibility.[88]

---

[88] Of course, this needn't stop with mere words. If we're able, we should also step into the actual situation where possible and appropriate, getting involved and solving problems.

I Will Lay Aside Power to Serve You

More than once, I've been struck with the sheer impracticality of the gospel. Of all the ways God could have revealed himself to us, he chose to become organic matter. Gestating in a womb. Slowly moving through the phases of human development. Living, dying, resurrecting. From a human perspective, it seems the least logical choice for a redemption plan. And yet, that is what God has done. In coming to earth and becoming a baby, Jesus left his seat at the right hand of the Father. He voluntarily descended to live, walk, sleep, and eat alongside those he loved and served. He cried for them. Washed their feet. Cooked for them. He moved through the world in a way that baffled his family, his followers, his friends, and his foes. As we've seen, he was willing to say what needed to be said, no matter the consequences.

And yet there are those among us—those called to walk in his steps—who have avoided something as simple as an awkward conversation because we're concerned about what it might cost us:

- Relationships.
- Social standing.
- Public affirmation.
- Leadership positions.

We know this could happen because we've seen it play out time and time again, in both our own social circles and in the broader culture.

Expressing an unpopular or opposing political viewpoint from that of our community can, at the very least, lead to a chilling effect in relationships and personal connections. At the worst, those who go against the flow see themselves excluded from opportunities, looked over, or pushed out. But considering the example Jesus left us to follow, I really don't see that those consequences should stop us.

I Will Do Things for You that You Cannot Do for Yourself

For a variety of factors—personality, temperament, precarious societal positions, and vulnerability—not everyone has the same ability to raise difficult questions. Nor do they even bear the same levels of responsibility. The stronger and more stable your position, the more respected your voice, the higher your position of responsibility, power, and authority, the greater your share of the burden in pressing through discomfort and engaging tough conversations. To whom much is given, much more is expected.[89] This is why throughout Scripture, we see calls for those with power, comfort, and authority to take up the cause of the poor, the weak, and the oppressed. Because they have no status and cannot help themselves, we mirror the gospel when we are willing to say, "Because you cannot speak for yourself, I will speak for you."

---

[89] Luke 12:48.

I Am Willing to Suffer for Your Sake

Awkward conversations are draining. How many of us avoid them even when they're clearly called for with justifications like these?

- I just don't have the energy today.
- I don't feel like dealing with that.
- Not opening that can of worms.
- It's not my problem.

While there may be circumstances in which it's appropriate to let something go, the problem is when these internal responses become habitual. When that happens, our silence becomes chronic, and we fail to take up our God-given responsibilities, which include preaching the word and being prepared in times both favorable and unfavorable to patiently correct, rebuke, and encourage people with good teaching.[90]

Not Everything Is a Debate

Perhaps many of us tap out of political discussions because too often they wind up morphing into debates. Instead of coming together to understand one another, we frequently set out to prove ourselves, establish our viewpoint as the correct one, and focus on

---

[90] 2 Timothy 4:2.

scoring points against our conversation partners rather than participating in fruitful dialogue with them.

If you're anything like me, nothing triggers your "Well Actually" self quite like political discourse. In order to keep every discussion from devolving into an entrenched debate, consider employing the steps we discussed in Chapter 3. When talking to someone who shares differing political views, make it a goal to try for five questions or intensifying statements in a row before pivoting to your own viewpoint—if you pivot at all. In understanding others better, you may find either 1) that your viewpoint isn't as firmly defensible as you thought or that 2) your comfortable talking points are aimed to combat thoughts and ideas the person you're talking to doesn't actually hold.

Of all the topics this book addresses, this one hits me the hardest. I find political discussions incredibly difficult and frustrating—not to mention super awkward. For many years, I avoided them completely. I told people "I just don't do politics."

That was not only wrong—it wasn't even the truth. I just didn't like talking about politics because such conversations always made me furious, and I looked for any cop-out I could take.

But over time, I've found that even though it's costly, it's still worth it to press through the awkwardness and engage this tough topic directly. There's just too much at stake.

The goal in talking politics isn't always to prove a point. It isn't necessarily to change minds to our way of thinking. It's not even to point out the error in the opinions of others, the candidate we don't like, or the party that has disappointed us.

The goal with these discussions is to break down the walls of misunderstanding, offense, and resentment that conversations about politics can erect. We do that by sincerity in our listening, by patience in our reactions, and by compassion in our responses.

We Are All One Body

In God's plan, we all need each other. We need intellectual, spiritual, and relational cross-pollination. This cross-pollination can both strengthen our previously held convictions and challenge faulty assumptions. Remember, a commitment to lifelong learning is a commitment to own up to areas in which we've been wrong or uninformed up to this point.

We need to hear opposing viewpoints directly from the people in our lives, not from media personalities who have a public platform with a personal agenda who try to tell us what those people believe. As someone who reads widely and sustains a broad media intake, let me say that the amount of misrepresentation and mischaracterization I see across the board are as overwhelming as they are disappointing. There's often a gap between what is *assume*d people believe and what they actually believe. Filling that gap is vital because in it, we may find space to come together— not necessarily to agree but to understand more where others are coming from and what's really motivating them. They, in turn, can hear us out and understand what we really think and believe and why. This can create a rich and fertile ground for spiritual formation if we're willing to meet, bring our tools, and till this patch of land together.

These are the sorts of conversations that can change hearts

even if they don't change minds. They help us see that although we may not agree in some areas, those disagreements don't need to make us mortal enemies. But they're not possible if we're not talking to each other. If we're not willing to meet, walk the property line, and mend fences.

Pressing through discomfort to engage people with social and political differences is never easy. It's generally awkward—especially awkward to start—but if the end results are worth it, then it's worth taking the risk.

Start Your Own Awkward Conversation

Find some trusted conversation partners for discussion or consider the questions on your own.

1. Do you tend to engage in political discussions or avoid them? Why is this your tendency?

2. Consider a political conversation you remember directly avoiding. What caused you to avoid engaging? Do you see this as a legitimate reason?

3. Discuss this statement: "Even people of faith often define themselves more in terms of what they're against than what they're for." What do you think creates this dynamic? Is this healthy or unhealthy?

4. Consider the gap between what you think the other side

thinks and what they actually think. How could such a gap wreak havoc on helpful political discourse? How can we close that gap?

5. How does the framework of the gospel affect your willingness to engage in awkward conversations of all sorts (including politics)?

6. What can be gained by being open and willing to have awkward political conversations?

Socially Awkward

Welcome to Awkwardsville:
At the Tips of My Fingers

Late winter in 2020, right before the Coronavirus pandemic took hold of the United States, my friend Lucy came to visit for a week. I planned the most Florida trip possible. Hot sun and iced coffees. Sunrise over the Atlantic, climbs to the tops of lighthouses, and airboat rides through alligator-infested waters. Sandhill cranes stalking with graceful precision. Lizards flitting ahead of us down the sidewalks. Flotillas of retirees sunning themselves. Plus, a long-haired septuagenarian stomping past us on the beach and yelling nonsense directly into our faces. All the classic Florida stuff.

On the night Lucy arrived, as we sat on a set of wooden steps overlooking the Intracoastal Waterway and waited for our table to open up at a downtown seafood restaurant, I grazed my hand along the step and picked up a rather largish splinter. It stabbed deep. My finger bled a bit. I dug around at it for a few minutes, even trying to shave it out with my credit card the way you do bee stingers. Then we were called for seating, and I forgot all about my splinter because our waiter was so deeply strange.

There was nothing technically wrong with him. He was fresh-faced and friendly. He took our orders without writing anything down and delivered exactly what we asked for. He was smiling and attentive. So smiling. So attentive.

It wasn't just that he kept our glasses filled and responded to our needs and maintained eye contact the whole time. It was the extreme level of eye contact.

From our very first, he came in hot—leaning in, opening his eyes wide, and staring directly into our faces at all times. Or perhaps it was our souls.

At the end, as I was paying the bill, he asked if I have a sister who lives in town.

Here we go, I thought. And also, *what a relief.*

This happens sometimes and was perhaps a reason behind all the smiling strangeness. I do, in fact, have a sister in town. She lives close to that very restaurant, and she's well-known and well-liked in the community. I've had people I had never met peg me as her relative before.

That must be it. He knows Bethany. He's going to ask if we're twins.

We're not, by the way. And he didn't.

Instead, he said, "You just look so much like my best friend's mom."

Reader, I am not his best friend's mom—despite the fact that his friend's mom is also named Ruth (of course she is). I'm not anyone's mom, for that matter. And judging by his age, I would have to be about fifteen years older than I am to make such a thing even biologically possible.

Lucy and I still aren't sure if that's what caused our waiter's strange and intense eye contact or if he's just like that all the time. Perplexed by all this, I completely forgot about my splinter. I went home, pried out my contact lenses, and crawled into bed completely oblivious.

In the morning, however, I woke to a slow, pulsing heat in my right hand, the pad of my splintered finger now discolored and inflamed. The only thing to do was to pull the splinter out, the sooner the better. Which meant before coffee.

I tip-toed around my studio apartment, silently opening and closing doors, leaving the lights off so that I wouldn't wake Lucy.

As the sun rose, I was standing directly beside one of my windows, tilting my finger into the early sunlight, searching for a good angle. I had not yet put in my contacts and was sporting a clunky and outdated pair of oversized librarian glasses. Like any reasonable middle-aged woman with a splinter trapped in her finger, I had also retrieved my half-size reading glasses from my desk, perched them onto the tip of my nose directly in front of my other glasses, and got to work.

Lucy woke to behold me silhouetted in a shaft of early morning sunlight, fingers inches from my face, snorting and grimacing as I squinted through two sets of glasses.

"I'm picking at my splinter," I told her, before she could even ask.

She blinked. Slowly. "Do you want some help?"

"Don't worry." I stabbed at my finger and pulled my head back, angling for the right distance to leverage the power of both sets of glasses. "I can get it."

"Ruth," Lucy said. "Remember. In God's plan, we all need each other."

CHAPTER 8
Of Such Is the Kingdom

At the time of this writing, I'm forty-two years old, and I am unmarried and childless. It's definitely not what I planned. Long-term singleness and childlessness through middle age is neither what I imagined or have ever desired. And yet here I am, dealing not only with the reality of my situation but also with everyone's perceptions, questions, and comments about it.

"Why are you still single?"

I'm not single because I'm awkward, but it's definitely awkward being single. As I mentioned in *The Proper Care and Feeding of Singles*, my 2017 book exploring singleness and the church, when people find out I'm still not married at this questionable age, they generally launch into a specific set of questions:

- You're not married?
- Why aren't you married?

- Did you ever want to be married?
- Do you think you ever will get married?
- What's wrong with all these guys?

I've addressed how I cope with such questions in that book.[91] For now, I just want to underscore how fundamentally awkward it feels to have complete strangers grilling me on such personal matters in public the first time we meet—usually in front of an audience.

We generally don't ask people about the details of their marriages, divorces, or wayward children during getting-to-know-you chit chats. And yet with singles, it seems to be open season on their personal lives.

Of course, we don't just do this to our singles. Anyone who doesn't seemingly fit the mold will recognize this situation. In particular, couples coping with infertility, miscarriage, and undesired childlessness are often grilled in very similar ways.

- Oh, you don't have children?
- Why don't you have any children?
- Do you ever want to have children?
- Do you think you ever will have children?
- You two had better get busy!

I'm not saying we shouldn't talk to couples about issues of

---

[91] Ruth Buchanan. *The Proper Care and Feeding of Singles: How Pastors, Marrieds, and Church Leaders Effectively Support Solo Members*, Write Integrity Press, 2017, 42.

infertility. As a matter of fact, from what I understand, this is a lonely and isolating experience, and a time when they could benefit from increased comfort and support. While some of that will come through measures such as the offer of meals and other practical services, conversation and compassionate counsel can go a long way toward helping couples feel as if they're not alone.

The entire premise of this book is that we should press through discomfort to engage tough topics. That being said, if this book has taught us nothing else so far, there's a time and a place and a proper mode of approach to take when engaging with difficult subjects. That includes singleness, childlessness, and infertility.

The very fact that people ask flippant questions such as the ones listed above means we absolutely should be talking about these things more—not less.

We Need to Talk

Marriage and childrearing are foundational to flourishing societies and rightly valued within the church. However, the church sometimes becomes so focused on marriages and families that it overlooks the experiences of those who are either not married or who are not bringing up children. It's as if we've forgotten that Jesus, the Author and Finisher of our faith, was himself a single man who never fathered a child. That many of the remarkable acts of faith in Scripture were carried out by the widows and the childless.

In her book *Longing for Motherhood*, author Chelsea Patterson Sobolik describes the moment when, at age nineteen, she discovered she would never carry a child. She'd just been diagnosed with a rare condition that caused her never to develop a uterus, and she was left stunned, grappling with feelings of sadness, frustration, grief, anger, shame, and loneliness.[92]

When I read Sobolik's book, I think about all the negative messages that can come from well-meaning but sadly misinformed people.

- "Just relax—I'm sure it will happen for you eventually."
- "Stop trying so hard."
- "I've heard when people adopt, they often wind up conceiving naturally."
- "Maybe God is trying to get your attention about something else first."
- "You need to let go and let God."

Of course, none of these would be appropriate to say to someone in Sobolik's situation—so why do some people assume they can deploy them as blanket responses? None of us knows what's really going on in people's lives, and we should be very careful not to speak as if we do.

Sobolik could have followed through on those and other suggestions to evoke a response from God for her "unanswered prayer," and she would still have remained childless. For couples in situations similar to Sobolik's, their pain is actually exacerbated

---

[92] Chelsea Patterson Sobolik. *Longing for Motherhood: Holding on to Hope in the Midst of Childlessness* (Chicago: Moody Publishers, 2018), 28.

by such well-meaning and yet thoughtless comments.

Which is not to say that everyone who deals with infertility is constantly in pain. The childless and infertile are not a monolith. They experience a broad range of emotions that we can't assume we understand from the outside.

In writing about her own experiences with childlessness, Professor Karen Swallow Prior has stated:

> That term, *infertile*, may be medically and technically appropriate, but it's not a word I would use to describe my life. A friend recently asked my advice for someone struggling with being infertile.
>
> "I'm not sure," I told her. "Because I don't really struggle with it at all."
>
> Even though God has not fulfilled my longtime desire to have children, he has filled my life with so many other gifts that my greatest struggle has been to be a faithful steward of so much abundance.[93]

When I first read her comments, my eyebrows spiked. I'd never heard a woman say anything like that before—perhaps because, at least in my generation, infertility and childlessness is something we rarely—if ever—openly discuss.

---

[93] Karen Swallow Prior. "The Hidden Blessing of Infertility." *CT Women.* https://www.christianitytoday.com/ct/2014/july-august/hidden-blessing-of-infertility.html (Accessed April 2, 2021).

Something to Talk About

While 8% of couples who seek treatment for infertility find that the male is the only identifiable cause, 12% of all women have difficulty conceiving and carrying a pregnancy to term.[94] Though many treat infertility and childlessness as primarily a woman's problem, we know deep down that it's certainly anything but. Nor is it even necessarily a couple's problem. Long-term singles who desire marriage and family and yet find themselves aging out of their childbearing years may experience related emotional journeys.

I was shocked when I first learned that between 10-20% of all known pregnancies end in miscarriages. For much of my life, miscarriages were never mentioned around me. Growing up in conservative church circles in the 80s and 90s, sitting through every Sunday morning and Sunday night service and every Wednesday prayer meeting that took place, I can't remember a time when we prayed for a couple who had lost a child in this way. In most cases, couples grieved privately, maybe telling a few family members or close friends. Open grief, mourning, or public acknowledgment of these losses rarely took place in my community.

As I moved through my 20s and 30s, and my friends and church peers married and started families, this trend continued. Occasionally, in hushed tones, someone would mention that

---

[94] "Infertility FAQ's." The Centers for Disease Control. https://www.cdc.gov/reproductivehealth/infertility/index.htm (Accessed April 2, 2021).

they—or someone we knew—had lost a baby. These losses are understandably emotional and intensely personal. But the trend of complete silence does seem to be changing. Those in the Millennial and GenZ generations do seem to be much more open to sharing their grief. Perhaps this is part of the overall push toward community and authenticity that's been taking place in my corner of Christianity over the last twenty years.

For whatever reason, the tide does seem to be shifting. Whether this sea change is cultural, generational, or some blend of the two, people are beginning to speak more openly and candidly about matters related to infertility, pregnancy loss, and unfulfilled longings.

Dr. Jessica Zucker, a psychologist specializing in maternal mental health, experienced the loss of her second pregnancy. When she didn't receive much comfort from her close circle, she wrote this:

> Pregnancy loss is not a disease that can be cured; it's not going anywhere—it is, in fact, a normative outcome of pregnancy. And it is therefore a topic we would benefit from engaging in candidly and integrating into everyday conversations, devoid of silence, stigma, and shame. To help ourselves and to help future generations. To normalize the experience, its aftermath, and the grief that flows from it. To allow those of us who have gone through it to be simultaneously vulnerable about our circumstances

and lovingly embraced for it.[95]

Given the statistics, many of you reading will either have suffered a pregnancy loss, experienced infertility, or been close to someone else who has. Or like me, you may be a single person whose hopes of marriage and family have not come to fruition.

My goal here isn't to force those who have grieved or are currently grieving to talk about it more. There are likely seasons when you feel more or less able to be forthright on these matters. Instead, I'd like to take a moment to address those among us who have not. When these topics do arise, those of us who have not dealt with them directly need to address them in a way that doesn't cause undue pain.

The Tension

For those of us in the church, here's the tension we face: we must walk the line of knowing how best to affirm the goodness of marriage, family, and children while still talking sensibly about singleness, infertility, miscarriage, and childlessness. It's honestly not as hard as you might think, especially when you understand that those experiences are not necessarily opposed to one another but are instead realities the people in your community are experiencing alongside one another. Most of the hurt in these conversations arises when in the rush to affirm marriage and

---

[95] Jessica Zucker. *I Had a Miscarriage: A Memoir, A Movement* (New York: Feminist Press, 2021), 27.

family, the realities of the faithful single or childless are overlooked or outright disparaged.

I've endured this particular brand of pain so many times it's hard to pick just one example. But there is one that was particularly hurtful. I sat through a service in which the pastor characterized all single women in my current age bracket as those who, in their twenties and thirties, had not gotten married because we wanted to have fun, enjoy life, pursue careers, and "do our own thing"—and in doing so, had turned our backs on God's will for our lives, squandering our opportunities to marry and now reaping the fruit of our self-centered choices.

Let me assure you, there's a way to affirm marriage and family as part of God's plan and good for society and the world without assuming that everyone who's not married at my age is automatically selfish and going astray. Likewise, there's a way to tenderly approach talking about childlessness that doesn't rest on faulty assumptions and deepen wounds.

Remember, those who are not married or raising children are not in a category marked "other." They're not enemies of these good gifts. In fact, many of them desperately desire these for themselves. They're simply experiencing something else alongside those who are married and raising children.

Pressing Through

When we're not able to come together to discuss issues of singleness, childlessness, infertility, we lose out. Many among us who have experienced these situations have learned so much about maintaining faith in the face of unfulfilled longings. The depth of our suffering and faith can add richness to our understanding of the goodness of God.

By pressing through discomfort to engage socially awkward conversations regarding singleness, childlessness, and unfulfilled longings, we gain access to the wisdom and richness of others' spiritual experiences. And, more importantly, we gain key insights into how these circumstances are affecting our siblings in Christ. When we understand them better as individuals, we're in a much better position to love and serve them in the best way possible.

Moving Forward and Looking Back

Maya Angelou has said, "Do the best you can until you know better. Then when you know better, do better."[96] I love the grace in that statement. But I'd like to take it one step further. When you learn better, don't just do better moving forward—take time to apologize for the mistakes of the past.

After my book *The Proper Care and Feeding of Singles* released, one of my close married friends called me. After telling me what she'd learned about caring for singles by reading my book, she told me that the book helped her make sense of a strange incident she'd had with a fellow single friend of ours years ago. "I never understood why he got so upset with me back then," she confided. "But now I get it."

---

[96] Megan Angelo. "16 Unforgettable Things that Maya Angelou Wrote and Said." *Glamour. https://www.glamour.com/story/maya-angelou-quotes* (Accessed August 10, 2021).

What she'd learned from the book shed new light on some comments she'd made to him, and now she understood how they had hurt him. She asked if I thought she should go back and apologize, or if I thought he'd likely forgotten about it.

I told her if she remembered, he remembered. And even if he didn't, that wouldn't necessarily ease the burden of her responsibility to make amends.

We're all on an arc of personal and spiritual growth, and we need to be willing to cut ourselves and our fellow wayfarers some slack. When you learn better, do better, and if you're able to circle back and make things right, do so. In the same vein, be willing to listen when others circle back to you. These conversations may not be easy. But the rewards of pressing through to engage them is well worth the small price of temporary discomfort.

Start Your Own Awkward Conversation

Find some trusted conversation partners for discussion or consider the questions on your own.

1. Describe a time when you witnessed someone ask seemingly flippant questions or make insensitive comments about singleness, childlessness, or infertility.

2. Discuss this statement from the chapter: "The childless and infertile are not a monolith." How should this form our perspectives?

3. As we press through discomfort to engage these topics, why is it vital that we proceed with caution? How can we adjust our mindset to ensure that we effectively consider those who have been hurt or may be experiencing this ongoing pain as a result of similar circumstances?

4. Why is it worth it to press through discomfort and engage in awkward conversations regarding singleness, childlessness, and unfulfilled longings?

Welcome to Awkwardsville:

Exercise in Humility

One night, after a particularly hard class at the gym, a group of us stood around complaining in that satisfied-but-irritated way people do when they've just done something tremendously hard and are now feeling both proud and indignant. We stood near the lockers, gathering our possessions, complaining, and sweating.

One of our coaches commented on my execution of a particularly nasty exercise, the Crab Walk Toe Tap. His affirmation came as a pleasant surprise. Since I'm not known for my balance or agility, I have struggled in the past to execute this maneuver without toppling over. I basked in the praise, taking it personally in the best possible way.

As all my coaches know, I'm not young, have never been any good at physical challenges, and hate working out. To top it all off, I started my getting-fit phase later in life, which means I have no rosy memories of youthful accomplishment to fall back on. Nor does my body have any reliable muscle memories to carry me through. At this point, I take any win I can get.

As I thanked the coach for noticing, a stranger lurched into view, approaching our group from the back. Perhaps he was waiting to get his stuff from the lockers. Maybe he just wanted to make a friend. Whatever his motives, he failed to sense the lay of the land before inserting himself into the conversation.

My coach was just saying that my Crab Walk Toe Taps had looked really solid when this man arrived. Flicking his eyes up and down my small frame, he smirked. "Just you wait, honey. Things will change when you hit forty."

My blood rose to an instant boil. I squared my stance, facing him fully and eyeing him from the top of his sweaty head to the tips of his joggers.

I arched a brow. "And how old are you?"

"I'm forty."

"Son," I laughed, flipping my bag over my shoulder, "I'm older than you are."

I turned on my heel and marched to the door, throwing a peace sign over my shoulder to the sound of a surprised burble of laughter from the group.

Once in the car, the boiling eased, and I simmered into a toxic stew of sweat and regret. Why had I felt the need to flatten that man so tremendously? And in front of an audience? It's not his fault genetics have smiled upon me, and I look a full decade younger than I actually am. Or that I write dialogue for a living, lending me a hidden access to snappy comebacks. Too snappy, maybe.

I squirmed, chewing my lip. Being able to casually roast the life out of anyone you choose is a double-edged sword. Just because you can doesn't mean you should. The next time I saw him, I would apologize, crack a few jokes about good genetics, and make it right. Better to humble myself now than be humbled later by circumstance.

Unfortunately, to this day, I've never seen him at the gym again.

Socially Awkward

CHAPTER 9
When We Are Weak

There's something wrong with my body. That's why although I've never been pregnant, I sleep with a therapeutic maternity pillow. If you ever take the time to look at me—I mean truly look closely, you'll notice. My shoulders sit off-kilter, my spine curves, my hips tilt. This isn't just an issue of appearance, however; it results in chronic pain.

I'm certainly not alone. An estimated 20% (50 million) of U.S. adults experience chronic pain. Women and older adults tend to suffer the most occurrences of chronic pain, but among those fifty million people, you'll find a wide variety of individuals, old and young, women and men, rich and poor, bankers and farmers and kindergarten teachers.[97] We're everywhere. With 20% of our population dealing with some level of chronic pain, one in five people that you know suffers from it. They sit beside you at church,

---

[97] Dahlhamer J, Lucas J, Zelaya, C, et al. Prevalence of Chronic Pain and High-Impact Chronic Pain Among Adults — United States, 2016. MMWR Morb Mortal Wkly Rep 2018;67:1001–1006.https://www.cdc.gov/mmwr/volumes/67/wr/mm6736a2.htm (Accessed May 12, 2021).

hang out with you on the weekends, and work long shifts alongside you. Some of them just talk about the issues more than others.

Keeping Up Appearances

A few years ago, when teaching a women's Bible study at my former church in Florida, I realized that most people in my life didn't know I deal with chronic pain. Despite the fact that I'm an extrovert who loves attention, this was one area of my life I'd been relatively quiet about. Because people didn't know about my pain, they weren't praying for me. They weren't looking out for me on bad days. They just didn't know. I knew this situation was my own doing since I hadn't really told many people. I had to grapple with asking when, why, and how this shroud of mystery had developed.

Certainly, some of this is down to my personal pride. Deep down, I feel most comfortable when I am able to maintain a strong façade. Anything that would potentially weaken me in the eyes of others makes me extremely uncomfortable. But God's been working with me in this area. Even beyond that, however, there's something else in play. Another reason lurking in the background. It's not just that I don't want to talk about my pain. It's that I don't like where the conversation invariably goes when I do.

A Pain in the Neck

In the past, I've been hesitant to bring up my chronic condition for several reasons. It's a relatively low-level problem compared to what some people deal with. And I've been managing my condition my entire adult life. For the past few years, due to therapy, physical training, and adaptions like sleeping with a maternity pillow, I've come to enjoy a season of relative ease. So, I don't feel the need to mention it all the time.

Still, I've found that (barring few exceptions) discussing chronic pain with people who have not suffered in similar ways invariably leads to a flurry of well-meaning suggestions. People jump to recommend everything from meditation to massage to chiropractic to electrical impulse devices to essential oils. Yes, I've tried everything, and I know you mean well and are trying to care for me, but we really don't need to have this discussion right now. I'm trying to tell you about my pain, and you're trying to solve it in real-time, something not even my doctors have been able to do.

The main reason I rarely discuss my pain in public—the reason that's most pertinent to our discussion in this book—is that over time, I realized that many of my fellow Christians don't know how to react to this aspect of life.

When I tell people I suffer with chronic pain, they will often respond in one of the following ways:

- Run through a litany of the aforementioned recommendations
- Ask if I've prayed to be healed
- Wonder if God is trying to teach me something
- Hint that I may have unresolved spiritual issues/unconfessed sin

Other writers—deeper theologians than I—have explored the intersection of faith and physical pain. For our purposes, it's not necessary that we wade those deep waters. Instead, I'd like to discuss how we can make these conversations infinitely less awkward for all of us.

Affirm and Ask

When someone tells you about their chronic pain issues, your first and primary response should be to listen. Though your first instinct will be to jump in and make suggestions—you want to do something to help—one of the best things you can do for your suffering friend is to listen well.

Some sort of response is called for, of course. That's the nature of conversation. Rather than suggestions, I recommend a combination of affirming their pain and asking good questions.

- SAY: That sounds frustrating.
- ASK: Have you noticed any ways that your pain and suffering has shaped you?
- SAY: Wow, I really respect how you're handling it.
- ASK: What have you learned about life by going through this?
- SAY: I'm so sorry you have to deal with that.
- ASK: How has this experience affected your understanding of the goodness of God?
- SAY: I wish this weren't happening to you.

- ASK: Have you found anything that seems to help?

As a chronic pain sufferer, I'd much rather respond to questions or comments like these than have my faith immediately questioned and/or be asked if I've tried a foam roller and peppermint oil. This approach will no doubt feel awkward at first. But in the long run, these sorts of conversations could prove more productive.

It's not that I think we shouldn't be talking about pain, or that there isn't a time and a place to share helpful tools that may bring relief. I actually think we should be talking about these issues more rather than less, especially in cases where there may actually be no solutions, cures, or fixes.

Facing It Head-On

I'd like to think that my issue with discussing my chronic pain is a personal problem unconnected from the larger evangelical landscape. However, the further back I step and the more I lean back to take in the big picture, the clearer I see that my response fits into a broader pattern. We're good at talking about the answered prayers, the blessings, the wins, and the victories. We're slower to publicly acknowledge the losses, the unanswered prayers, the pain, and the insufficiencies.

As I've mentioned before, pride is certainly part of my issue here. But there's something deeper at work—something tied to theology. In some corners of our faith communities, having a testimony plagued with pain, loss, and devastation poses a major theological problem. If our God is a god of miracles, healings, and happy endings, what do we do with people whose journeys don't line up with our notion of a happily ever after? What do we make of the pain that doesn't go away, the sicknesses that linger or lead to death, the weak, the ill, and disabled? Either there's something wrong with this view of God, or there's something wrong with these people.

Waiting on a Miracle

While the God of the Bible does work miraculously, and we do see instances of healing and happy endings, we also witness a spiritual reality that is infinitely more complex. We follow a risen Savior, yes. One who literally came back from the dead. But as his nail-scarred hands remind us, he intentionally laid down his life, not sparing himself from pain and suffering. Instead, he embraced it, working a mysterious good through it. To believe that a mark of God's favor is to live a pain-free life and that anything less is a sign of his displeasure is to fall victim to a theological myth—one that has flourished particularly in the United States, largely due to the nature of the comfortable lifestyles many of us enjoy.

Calling this the myth of "American Christian exceptionalism," Professor Soong-Chan Rah explains that "American Christian exceptionalism contributes to a triumphalism that focuses on a narrative of success and victory. When suffering occurs, it's considered a hindrance to the work of God in the world. The narratives of suffering communities, therefore, are considered to be inferior and are ignored or removed from the dominant narrative of triumph."[98]

That's why our evangelical conferences tend to feature big-name speakers from large churches with big budgets and splashy programming, prioritizing them over smaller, deeper, and often more effective community-rooted ministries. This dominant narrative of success can quickly take root in our subconscious evaluation of our own spirituality, convincing us that if we're not winning, our faith must not be working.

This thinking couldn't be further from the truth. It's in our weakness that the power of Christ rests on us, and through our brokenness that God's glory rests powerfully on our lives. We must never lose sight of the fact that while Christ rose from the dead, he still *died*—he was buried and lay three days in the grave, his body horribly disfigured. And when he returned, he carried scars that he will bear through eternity.

> Christ bears the nail marks even on his post-resurrection new body. The carrying over of the wounds of Christ from the old creation to the new marks a startling portal from which to consider the link between what we do on this side of eternity and what we do on the other side.
>
> Our wounds matter to God, as they are

---

[98] Soong-Chan Rah, "Evangelical Futures," in *Still Evangelical: Insiders Reconsider Political, Social, and Theological Meaning*, ed. Mark Labberton (Downer's Grove: Intervarsity Press, 2018), 84.

connected with Christ's sacrifice.[99]

As in all things, Christ has left for us an example here. He did not try to hide his wounds but instead invited others to come and look—even to touch them. And why would he hide them? They were a sign and a symbol of a miraculous work.

"Do not disbelieve," Jesus says, pointing directly to his scars. "But believe."[100]

While in the past I shied away from talking about my pain, I now seek to address it naturally when appropriate. To invite people close and allow them to bear witness. Yes, it's generally awkward, especially when I turn aside the suggestion that I invest in a hot tub. Instead of short-circuiting these conversations in an effort to avoid frustration, I now point the conversation toward the Suffering Servant himself, and what his pain has taught me about enduring my own.

All in the Family

Up to this point, my observations have addressed how chronic conditions can be approached on a personal level. There is, however, another layer to this conversation—the church family dynamic. Most church families are adept in serving one another during single-event emergencies. When there's a new baby, a death in the family, accidents, or a scary diagnosis, the family of

---

[99] Makoto Fujimura. *Art + Faith: A Theology of Making*. (New Haven: Yale University Press, 2020), 104.
[100] John 20:24-29.

God shows up. It's one of the things I loved most about my most recent church family. We absolutely knew how to take care of each other. Phone calls, texts, and food drops—these were both organized by committee and accomplished spontaneously outside the system. These practical modes of caring helped sufferers know that our church family sees us, understands our problems, and cares enough to express their love in practical ways.

While these are wonderful and necessary steps, they only seek to underscore the lack of care many church families express in the event of long-term suffering in their midst. While people are motivated to show up for short-term crises, they often exhibit remarkably less energy when it comes to serving and caring for one another over the long haul. When a member faces a sustained illness, an extended mental health challenge, or long-term chronic conditions—particularly ones that require them to be absent from corporate gatherings for an extended period of time—it doesn't take too long for them to feel as if they have fallen by the wayside. Texts peter out. Phone calls dwindle. Offers of meals and visits slow to a trickle—then to an occasional drip. While there's something to be said for the out-of-sight-out-of-mind effect, it also seems that there isn't much of a category in most of our frameworks for taking care of long-haulers, be they chronically ill, housebound, or disabled.

If this area of care is indeed a shortcoming in the function of many of our church bodies, then there may be an underlying reason why. Could it be that a shallow vision of God's purposes in pain limits our ability to serve—and even talk about—ongoing suffering?

Show Us the Way

As I've read and studied Scripture throughout my adult life, there are times that I've related both to Peter and to Paul. With Peter, every time he says something well-meaning but thoughtlessly impulsive, I cringe in shared embarrassment. Ours is a shared legacy of well-intentioned but impulsive wrong-headedness.

When I think about Paul, however, I feel more of a deep-seated recognition with a kindred spirit who has counted the cost of being real with himself and others. He knows that being a straight talker is going to upset people, but he also feels a bone-deep compulsion to do it anyway. This is the energy Paul brings to discussing pain, weakness, and shortcomings; and if we're ever going to get anywhere with this, I believe his example may show us a way forward.

As many of us are aware, Paul's journeys proved challenging, both because of the sometimes-violent nature of people's reaction to his message (beatings, stoning, imprisonment, shipwrecks, etc.) and because of a particular physical infirmity he mentions specifically in one of his letters. Some scholars actually connect Paul's turbulent missionary experience to his infirmity, proposing that Paul's poor physical condition, which he mentions in Scripture more than once, is likely the direct result of the violence to which he had been subjected.[101]

Either way, in writing his second letter to the church at

---

[101] N.T. Wright. *Paul: A Biography.* (San Francisco: HarperOne, 2018), 123.

Corinth, Paul demonstrates for them and for us what it looks like to publicly acknowledge ongoing infirmities, weakness, losses, and failures.

> But whatever anyone else dares to boast of—I am speaking as a fool—I also dare to boast of that . . . I am talking like a madman—with far greater labors, far more imprisonments, with countless beatings, and often near death. Five times I received at the hands of the Jews the forty lashes less one. Three times I was beaten with rods. Once I was stoned. Three times I was shipwrecked; a night and a day I was adrift at sea; on frequent journeys, in danger from rivers, danger from robbers, danger from my own people, danger from Gentiles, danger in the city, danger in the wilderness, danger at sea, danger from false brothers; in toil and hardship, through many a sleepless night, in hunger and thirst, often without food, in cold and exposure. And, apart from other things, there is the daily pressure on me of my anxiety for all the churches. Who is weak, and I am not weak? Who is made to fall, and I am not indignant? If I must boast, I will boast of the things that show my weakness.[102]

---

[102] 2 Corinthians 11:21-30.

In the same letter, Paul acknowledges his ongoing physical infirmity, what he calls a "thorn in the flesh." While he posits that this problem has been sent from Satan to hurt him, God was nevertheless overruling and using it to keep him from being proud.

> Three times I pleaded with the Lord about this, that it should leave me. But he said to me, "My grace is sufficient for you, for my power is made perfect in weakness." Therefore I will boast all the more gladly of my weaknesses, so that the power of Christ may rest upon me. For the sake of Christ, then, I am content with weaknesses, insults, hardships, persecutions, and calamities. For when I am weak, then I am strong.[103]

In laying bare his failures, struggles, and weaknesses, Paul shows us that rather than hiding our suffering, we can—and perhaps even should—bring it into the light. It's not a matter of who should be talking about suffering, but about the aspects of suffering to which each of us is uniquely positioned to speak. Because while we all might be suffering in seemingly disparate and often uneven circumstances, this truth remains: eventually, suffering comes to all of us. It's only a question of what it will be and when it will arrive and whether we're equipped to talk about it when it does.

---

[103] 2 Corinthians 12:8-9

What We Miss

In failing to helpfully address weakness, pain, and chronic issues among the body of Christ—both in our conversations and our actions—we're missing out on the richness of the collective human experience. We're also missing the full display of God's power and glory.

Remember, in God's plan, we all need each other. Only when those with different levels of spiritual, emotional, intellectual, and physical strength and weakness come together can we truly demonstrate what it looks like to live as a community in which strength is made perfect in weakness. To show, as Paul stated, how the power of Christ rests on us. For when we are weak, then we are strong.

Sharing the Load

Though it's challenging sometimes to be open and honest about our suffering, there's great value in pressing through discomfort to engage socially awkward conversations regarding chronic suffering.

- We're able to learn how to pray and care for people and minister more effectively to one another.
- We can share the load of lament with one another, crying out together in our suffering.
- We're able to give glory to God for sustaining us through

our struggle.

- We can help demolish the harmful myth of American Christian exceptionalism.
- We can come together collectively to share in the sufferings of Christ.

Finally, in sharing our weakness and our brokenness with one another, we can even more effectively participate in the exhortation recorded in Hebrews 10:25, when we are told not to forsake coming together, but instead to gather for mutual encouragement, looking forward together to the coming of Christ.

Start Your Own Awkward Conversation

Find some trusted conversation partners for discussion, or consider the questions on your own.

1. Why are conversations surrounding chronic conditions so awkward?

2. In what ways might a flawed theology be impacting our inability to come to grips with the chronic pain and suffering in our midst?

3. Think of a time when you heard someone speak openly about his/her chronic condition. What was your takeaway from that interaction?

4. In what specific ways do you and/or your church take chronic pain and ongoing conditions into account when planning ministry and outreach opportunities?

5. If you suffer with a chronic condition/chronic pain, what do you wish the people around you knew?

Socially Awkward

Welcome to Awkwardsville

The Not-Date

It happened one dark evening in autumn when it felt like the sun went down at noon. It was the end of an exhausting week, and since I was a schoolteacher at the time, once I was home for the evening, all snuggled down in my fuzzy socks, I had no desire to go back out. Somehow, though, my sister Bethany convinced me that we should have a Girl's Night Out with some friends.

When we all get together, I'm usually the first one to arrive. I was surprised, then, when I approached the host stand and was greeted with a smile of recognition. "Are you Ruth?"

" . . . Yes?" It came out as a question, reflecting my instant suspicion. There's no way I'd ever met this fresh-faced young man. How did he know my name? Even if my friends were already here, there's no way he would know who I was or whom I was meeting.

"Great," he chirped. He gathered a menu and some napkin-rolled silverware. "Your party is already here. Right this way."

Alarm bells chimed softly in the back of my mind, but I ignored them. I'd lived in the same town since the late 1980s, heavily involved in the community through church and school. I was on the brink of asking the young host if he was the sibling of someone I'd taught, when he stopped next to a table for two.

"Here you go," he trilled, dropping my menu and silverware across from yet another total stranger.

"Who's this?" I asked the host.

"This is your party," he informed me, backing away.

"No, it's not."

I slanted my gaze at this new stranger. He was youngish and fairly good-looking. He leaned back in the wooden chair, one arm hooked over the top rail, shoulders crooked at an angle. He tipped his head and looked up in my general direction, though not exactly meeting my gaze.

"Who are you?" I asked.

"Diego." He smiled slightly. The arm stayed casually draped over the seat next to him. He made no move to rise.

"Well," I gestured in the direction that the host had gone. "he's obviously dropped me at the wrong table, so—"

"No." Diego shifted again, straightening up. "It's a date."

I stopped, mid heel-turn. "Excuse me?"

"It's a date," Diego repeated. His eyes flicked to mine, then away.

"This," I gestured, "is not a date. I'm here to meet my sister."

"Bethany," he confirmed.

Wait, what? I stepped closer. "How do you know Bethany?"

"She's setting us up," he shrugged. Though he didn't look happy about it.

I'm sure I didn't either. Everything about this felt off. Diego wasn't my type, for one thing. He was much too young. And if there's one thing Bethany would never do, it's waste my time. Besides which, I can smell lies a mile away.

And this whole thing stank.

"How do you know Bethany?" I stepped closer to the table, entering Diego's personal space, watching him closely.

He glanced left. "We work together. At the barn."

She worked at two. "Which one?"

"The one where she works."

What was going on here? It's obvious he didn't know the name of either barn where she—and apparently, he—worked. Lie on lie. But to what purpose?

I stepped back. "I know you're lying."

Beads of sweat popped out on his forehead. He looked off to the left again, as if hoping to be rescued or, at the very least, shown a cue card.

At that point, it must have been apparent to anyone observing that the jig was up. Which is why it did not surprise me when, seconds later, off to the left, three heads popped around the corner, all grinning maniacally.

One head was attached to Bethany. The other two belonged to our friends Joe and Alissa, who were there for moral support on behalf of the poor man quietly sweating at a table for two.

The whole thing was a set-up, of course, but not the sort you might be thinking. Though the main arc of this story is much too involved to detail here, Bethany and I had been engaged in a years-long prank battle, and this was her latest attempt to one-up me.

When I tell this story now, I always start it in the same way.

"Once, my sister Bethany tried to convince me I was on a blind date."

One thing we do know. I'll never be one of those naïve women in a movie trapped in situations when she's sure something's wrong but plays along anyway for fear of rocking the boat. Nope. Instead, I'm the one who makes poor Diego regret he ever agreed to help prank someone's sister.

I know for sure he regretted it, because when I saw him again a few years later at a wedding, he pretended not to recognize me. And I knew he was pretending. Because the minute I said hi, I saw him start to sweat.

CHAPTER 10
Day of the Dead

A few months ago, my father glued himself to a grave. It's not as strange as it sounds. In fact, the backstory is somewhat prosaic. While working as an associate at a local funeral home, my dad finds himself charged with ensuring that mausoleums are properly sealed when someone is buried in the above-ground crypt. This task he generally accomplishes with the aid of a heavy-duty glue. Add to that task a windy Florida day and a flapping suit jacket, and you have the perfect recipe for gluing yourself to a grave.

This story cracked me up, and I felt bad for laughing. We're not used to laughing about funerals. Even though we know every job has its behind-the-scenes hilarity, this levity feels wrong. This is partly due to the fact that we don't want to speak ill of the dead, and partly due to the fact that we don't want to acknowledge death at all.

Speaking of Death

People from different cultures and different time periods have always handled death differently. At a Haitian funeral, you may observe ritual wailing and praying, with bodies laid to rest in colorful above-ground mausoleums. After the funeral, friends and family will likely observe a mourning period lasting for over a week. In Scotland, the interment will generally be preceded by a wake, a period during which the body will be laid out for several days and attended by a family member at all times. Guests who come to pay respects may be offered food and drink. A bagpiper might accompany the processional to the graveside service, at which time the body will be laid to rest. Korean funerals tend to take place in funeral halls, with guests bowing to the deceased and to the family, offering condolence money to help the family offset funeral expenses, including the cost of cremation.

Our American burial traditions are currently less elaborate than many places in the world—and as a people, we tend not to plan ahead. In general, we live as if we'll never die. For instance:

- Two out of three American adults don't have a will.[104]
- Only 37% have shared their end-of-life wishes through some sort of advanced directive.[105]
- While over 62.5% of Americans feel it is important to communicate their funeral wishes to family members

---

[104] "2021 Wills and Estate Planning" *Caring.org.* https://www.caring.com/caregivers/estate-planning/wills-survey/ (Accessed April 28, 2021).
[105] Michelle Andrews. "Many Avoid End-of-Life Care Planning, Study Finds" *NPR.* https://www.npr.org/sections/health-shots/2017/08/02/540669492/many-avoid-end-of-life-care-planning-study-finds (Accessed April 28, 2021).

prior to their own death, only 21.4% have done so.[106]

Why the huge gaps?

Trying Not to Think About It

In his book *Being Mortal,* surgeon Atul Gawande grapples with the unavoidable realities of death and dying, all while acknowledging that modern medical practice has shaped not only how we think about these realities but also whether we're forced to think about them at all.

> As recently as 1945, most deaths occurred in the home. By the 1980s, just 17 percent did. Those who somehow did die at home likely died too suddenly to make it to the hospital . . . or were too isolated to get somewhere that could help. Across not just the United States but also the entire industrialized world, the experience of advanced aging and death has shifted to hospitals and nursing homes.[107]

As a result, Gawande writes, it wasn't until he himself had

---

[106] "Funeral Planning Not A Priority For Americans." *PRNewswire.* https://www.prnewswire.com/news-releases/funeral-planning-not-a-priority-for-americans-300478569.html (Accessed April 28, 2021).

[107] Atul Gawande. *Being Mortal: Medicine and What Matters in the End.* (New York: Picador, 2014), 6.

"crossed over to the other side of the hospital doors" and become a doctor that he actually saw someone die. Only then did the immense magnitude of death settle over him.[108] Up until that point, death had felt like a distant theory. Now, here was the reality.

"Out of sight, out of mind," as the saying goes. Considering the way American culture currently compartmentalizes death, shunting all traces away and setting aside very little time to mourn, we should not find it surprising that our ability to discuss death has all but vanished from the public sphere. Something inside us resists talking about death, perhaps because we don't even want to think about it.

The Resistance

As a writer, I'm very well aware of what Steven Pressfield calls The Resistance. The Resistance, as he describes it, is a negative, repelling force that is always at work within writers, attempting to distract them and keep them from sitting down to do the work of writing. It's not the writing that's hard, Pressfield posits. It's The Resistance. The Resistance is the enemy of the writer, and the battlefield is within their own minds.[109]

You don't have to be a writer to recognize this sort of force in play in your own life. We all experience times when we sense an inner barrier to expressing our thoughts and feelings—sometimes

---

[108] Ibid., 7.
[109] Steven Pressfield. *The War of Art: Break Through the Blocks and Win Your Inner Creative Battles* (New York: Black Irish Entertainment, LLC, 2002), 7, 87.

even a resistance so strong that it doesn't allow us to think our own thoughts or feel our own feelings on a particular matter. Yet in a case as important as this—the literal matter of life and death—we must seek to overcome The Resistance. There's too much on the line to pretend that death won't come for us. The reality simply must be dealt with.

Not talking about death won't keep it from happening to us. The only thing our silence will accomplish will be to make us less prepared to grieve, less prepared to comfort those who are mourning, and less prepared to die ourselves.

Prepare to Grieve

As a culture, Americans weren't always as cut off from traditions surrounding grief as they are now. Take, for example, the Victorians. Some would even say this generation was obsessed with death, and no wonder. Death was a frequent visitor to Victorian homes, and because dying was more often than not accomplished at home surrounded by friends and family members, most people's relationship with death was open and ongoing [110]

During this era, funeral practices were detailed and specific, and etiquette related to the mourning period was high. Strict social expectations governed how long one should mourn, for whom, and what precisely should be worn during each phase of a mourning

---

[110] Marilyn A. Mendoza, PhD. "Death and Mourning Practices in the Victorian Age," *Psychology Today*, *https://www.psychologytoday.com/us/blog/understanding-grief/201812/death-and-mourning-practices-in-the-victorian-age* (Accessed April 26, 2021).

period. Far from the common modern American habit of setting aside a few hours to attend a visitation or grave-side service (if we even do that), Victorians took months—and, in the case of full mourning, even years—to express their grief.

While some Victorian customs may seem morbid to us now—taking portraits of the deceased or weaving human hair into wreaths and jewelry—no one can accuse the Victorians of not being prepared to grieve. Meanwhile, those of us who lose a close family member today may be shocked to learn that because employment laws do not mandate bereavement leave, we may struggle with our employer to be granted adequate time off from our jobs to attend the funeral service, let alone find adequate space to grieve.

Prepare to Comfort

Throughout the year, I lead writing workshops for both fiction and non-fiction authors. Because I work with these writers over a period of several months, there are times when, in the natural course of life, they suffer the loss of close friends and family members. In fact, this happened to two of my workshop members just this week. They do not know one another, and the losses they've suffered are of a different nature; nevertheless, they are both grieving deeply. They both have close-knit local support systems on which to rely, and for that I'm thankful. They are not grieving alone.

Naturally, I excused them from all their workshop responsibilities, and I also actively encouraged them to write only if it's therapeutic and not to force themselves to work during their time of grief. I'm only able to admonish them in these ways, of course, because they told me of their loss. They reached out with their sad news, and I responded.

In the same way we're able to respond to news of a death, we could also respond to people's hopes, fears, wishes, and concerns regarding end-of-life issues. Unfortunately, in a culture uncomfortable with acknowledging death, we do not take the opportunities naturally presented to us.

If someone begins a sentence with "When I die—" and we immediately cut them off with "Oh, don't say that," we could be preventing some of the very conversations that would do us the most good.

Furthermore, when we immediately cut off conversations related to death and dying—sometimes with the admonition that the other person should "stop being morbid,"—we're communicating an underlying discomfort with a topic that, for the Christian, should hold little fear.

For the Christian, there is no fear in death. In fact, death has been swallowed up in victory. Some of us need to read Romans 8 again—perhaps even memorizing it, marinating our minds in the reality of the resurrection of the body and the promise of life everlasting.

The Romans 8 Mindset

In Romans chapter 8, Paul is calling upon Christians to reorient their perspectives, aligning their mindsets to match their new Kingdom realities.

The Romans 8 Mindset takes these truths to heart:

> For to set the mind on the flesh is death, but to set the mind on the Spirit is life and peace. For the mind that is set on the flesh is hostile to God, for it does not submit to God's law; indeed, it cannot. Those who are in the flesh cannot please God.
>
> You, however, are not in the flesh but in the Spirit, if in fact the Spirit of God dwells in you. Anyone who does not have the Spirit of Christ does not belong to him. But if Christ is in you, although the body is dead because of sin, the Spirit is life because of righteousness. If the Spirit of him who raised Jesus from the dead dwells in you, he who raised Christ Jesus from the dead will also give life to your mortal bodies through his Spirit who dwells in you.[111]

With the Spirit of God living in us, we belong not to the realm of death but to the realm of life and peace. When our mindsets are adjusted to this reality, we are prepared not only to discuss matters related to death and dying with confidence, but we're also in a wonderful position to comfort others. For Christian and non-Christian conversation partners alike, we can point them to the Resurrection of Jesus Christ and the promise that he is restoring all

---

[111] Romans 8:6-11.

things as the cause of our confidence and the foundation of our cheerful hope in the face of death.

The irony here is that while we may find it more comfortable not to talk about death, in submitting to that natural resistance, we avoid the very thing that would make us the most comfortable in the long run.

Prepare to Die

When asked how afraid they are to die, only 25% of Americans claimed they were not at all afraid to die. While 7% of those surveyed claimed not to know how they felt, the breakdown for the rest of the survey respondents was as follows:

- 11% Very Afraid
- 31% Somewhat Afraid
- 27% Not Very Afraid

While varying levels of fear are expressed here, these numbers point to something very real and very human: 69% of everyone we know, in one way or another, is afraid to die.[112] While this is certainly a contributing factor to why we don't like to talk about death very much, these high levels of fear could also be a direct result of not talking about death enough.

---

[112] "United States: How Afraid Are You of Death?" *Statista.* https://www.statista.com/statistics/959347/fear-of-death-in-the-us/ (Accessed April 28, 2021).

As followers of a resurrected Christ—one who defeated death and is the first fruits of the resurrection—talking about death should be no problem for us. I don't want to gloss over the pain and uncertainties associated with death and loss. We definitely might suffer as we die, some of us in excruciatingly painful ways. We have all already experienced the grief of separation associated with the death of loved ones, and we will experience it again. But we are also heirs of a new Kingdom, one in which death has no sting and the grave no ultimate victory. In adopting the quintessentially American out-of-sight, out-of-mind approach to death and grief—in not talking about it lest we make someone feel awkward or uncomfortable—are we reflecting a true Kingdom culture or a merely societal one?

Loss and Gain

When we refuse to talk about death and dying, here are some things we lose:

- Commiserating with our neighbors and connecting in real ways around a very human concern
- Admonishing fellow believers in the hope of the Resurrection
- Communicating our own end-of-life wishes, thereby removing the burden of future decision making from our grieving family members and friends
- Reflecting a true Kingdom mindset as we operate in

society

- Pointing those who fear death toward the hope of life everlasting

There's much to lose. But by pressing through discomfort to engage socially awkward conversations regarding grief, death, and dying, however, there is also much to gain. In my estimation, the rewards are worth the risk of a few awkward conversations.

Start Your Own Awkward Conversation

Find some trusted conversation partners for discussion or consider the questions on your own.

1. Why do so many Americans seem to avoid talking about death? In your experience, has that been the case?

2. Describe the last time you had an honest conversation with someone about death, dying, grief, or loss. What were the circumstances leading up to that discussion? What were the results?

3. What do we potentially lose by refusing to press through discomfort and engage awkward conversations about death and dying? What could we potentially gain by pressing through?

4. When we refuse to talk about death and dying, who suffers and in what ways?

Welcome to Awkwardsville

"I'll be right over there."

One of the best features of my former church is that it's extremely warm and welcoming. It's so small that newcomers are immediately noticeable.

One Sunday, I noticed a woman sitting all by herself against the back wall. Rather than installing pews, our church favors interlocking plush seats. She'd chosen one right along the aisle, "As if she were ready to dash at an instant's notice," I later told Bethany.

As people sometimes do when they're in the midst of a crowd of strangers, she sat stiffly, staring straight ahead, hands folded in her lap. She didn't look unapproachable. Just bored—and a bit blank.

I would fix that.

I trotted over and perched in the seat along the aisle just in front of hers, legs in the aisle, angling back to face her, torso twisted at the waist, and my hands on the chairback in front of her. "Hello!" I caroled directly into her face.

She smiled back coolly, receiving my introduction and

answering my basic questions. While her manner wasn't off-putting, she didn't seem overly chatty or excited to continue engaging. I welcomed her again, double-checked her name, and braced myself to stand and leave.

But here's the thing.

Saturday had been Leg Day at the gym. Incline sprints on the treadmill. A thousand-meter row. Goblet squats. Dumbbell thrusters. Some pop jacks. Having now been sitting for a good five minutes, I sensed mid-rise that my quads had stiffened up. Realizing I wasn't going to make it to my full, upright stance without a little help, I tightened my grip on the chairback in front of me, pulling slightly to use if for leverage. Which would have worked out fine had the chair been properly connected to its neighbor. Only it wasn't.

Free and independent from the row, the chair tilted in my hands, destabilizing me even further. I tottered mid squat on my stiff and uncompromising legs. My quads shrieked. Desperately trying to look normal, I released the chair, which tipped silently back into place. Knees still hinged, stiff joints seemingly locked in place, I took three hopping steps backward, eyes wide, maintaining eye contact with the guest the entire time—still smiling, lest she worry. I straightened my knees and rose to my full height.

The smile didn't seem to have the effect I'd hoped. "Are you okay?" the guest asked. Her eyebrows contracted sharply.

I babbled something—who knows what—trying to explain the situation to the guest and to everyone else sitting in the vicinity, who were now watching the encounter with interest. Never have I wished more for a man in a straw hat to tap-dance past and drag me off-stage with the hook of his cane.

This being reality, I would need to end the scene on my own. "Anyway," I said, beaming my full, toothy smile at the guest, "I'll be right over there." I pointed to where I usually sit. "If you need anything before you leave, that's where I'll be. Feel free to come find me."

Reader, she did not.

Socially Awkward

CHAPTER 11
Who Hurt You?

I might be too online for my own good. As a writer and author coach who currently works from home, I spend much of my day on the internet. I write and research. I chat on social media. I skim headlines and read articles. I host meetings on screens and play online word games. One thing people who are Very Online know is that the internet has its own version of slang. At one point, a popular way to respond when people saw someone reacting dramatically or overreacting to something small was to ask, "Who hurt you?"

I used to find this response funny. Then I learned the statistics on actual abuse. Not to be *that person* and take all our jokes away, but the reality is scary. Every nine seconds, a person in America is abused.[113] Many of us have someone who did, indeed, hurt us. That's no laughing matter, and the only reason I could joke about it so flippantly was that I just didn't know. Because we don't talk

---

[113] *The Center for Family Justice.* "Statistics." https://centerforfamilyjustice.org/community-education/statistics/ (Accessed December 19, 2019).

about it.

Speaking Up

I'm not putting pressure on trauma victims themselves. While there's definitely a place for you to tell your stories, should that be your desire when you feel ready, it's absolutely not your responsibility to educate the non-traumatized about abuse. In many cases, that would only traumatize you further, and that's the furthest wish from my mind. Instead, I'm asking those of us who have not experienced abuse to do something most of us don't want to do: we must bear the awfulness in mind.

I'll explain how we can do this a bit further on in this chapter. For now, we need to talk about the rampant physical, spiritual, emotional, and sexual abuse plaguing us. We can't fix what we won't discuss, and we can't discuss what we refuse to look at. We can't fight a hidden enemy, particularly if we're the ones helping the enemy stay hidden. While it would be more comfortable to bury our heads in the sand and pretend none of this affects us, that is both naïve and wrong. To believe abuse doesn't affect you unless you're the one abusing or personally being abused is not just a lie but a hard-hearted dereliction of our responsibility to bear one another's burdens. You can't bear a load if you're unaware your sibling in Christ is carrying one, and you can't fight a battle if you won't open your eyes and look at the enemy.

For the sake of those who have suffered in this way and those who haven't, we need to be willing to learn, to listen, to discuss, to speak up. If we're not willing to overcome our awkwardness—our fear—our discomfort—about looking the abuse problem in the face, we'll all be poorer as a result. And the abusers will be all the more free to carry on abusing.

We're Right Here

In my many years of teaching and counseling women, I can count on one hand the number of women who have articulated their abuse and specifically asked for help. I love and honor them. However, a peek at the staggering statistics on sexual assault in the United States convinces me that these women are only the very tip of the iceberg.

At the time of this writing, here's where the numbers stand:

- Every seventy-three seconds, an American is sexually assaulted.
- One out of every six women has been the victim of an attempted or completed rape.
- One in thirty-three men have likewise experienced an attempted or completed rape.[114]
- An estimated 13% of women and 6% of men have experienced sexual coercion in their lifetime (i.e., unwanted sexual penetration after being pressured in a

---

[114] Rape, Abuse & Incest National Network (RAINN), "Victims of Sexual Violence: Statistics," https://www.rainn.org/statistics/victims-sexual-violence (Accessed June 6, 2020).

nonphysical way); and 27% of women and nearly 12% of men have experienced unwanted sexual contact.

- Approximately one in twenty-one men reported that they were made to penetrate someone else during their lifetime; and most men who were made to penetrate someone else reported that the perpetrator was either an intimate partner or an acquaintance.[115]

- Nearly one in three women and one in four men have experienced sexual violence involving physical contact during their lifetimes.

- One in four girls and one in thirteen boys experience sexual abuse in childhood.

- The official numbers are likely an underestimate because many cases go unreported.[116]

Taken as a whole, these statistics are overwhelming. Whether we realize it or not, we all know people who have been sexually abused and assaulted. Some of us are those people. However, talking about sexual abuse is so excruciatingly painful that many victims never speak of what happened to them, either to file an official criminal report or simply to tell a friend or loved one. This isn't simply because they don't want to talk about it. In many

---

[115] Center for Disease Control and Prevention (CDC), "National Intimate Partner and Sexual Violence Survey," https://www.cdc.gov/violenceprevention/pdf/nisvs_executive_summary-a.pdf (Accessed August 11, 2021) .

[116] Centers for Disease Control and Prevention (CDC), "Sexual Violence Is Preventable," https://www.cdc.gov/injury/features/sexual-violence/index.html (Accessed June 6, 2020).

cases, they can't.

Traumatic Memories

In addition to the deep shame sexual abuse survivors experience, they often are unable to give a coherent account of the actual events surrounding their abuse. This is because traumatic memories are not stored in the same way as other memories. Rather than a narrative with a beginning, middle and end, traumatic memories are often incoherent and fragmentary.[117]

Additionally, traumatic memories don't feel like other memories. Instead, when they are recounted, the emotions and physical sensations attached to the memory are not experienced as distant events but are instead experienced as physical reactions in the present.[118] Even with all this going on, traumatized individuals may lack the ability to connect with their feelings or even describe them.[119]

The upshot of all this is that when sexual assault survivors tell their stories, the resulting testimonies tend to seem, on the surface, to lack emotional consistency and cohesion. In a word, they may seem unbelievable.

My point is certainly not that we should be trying to pry stories out of sexual assault survivors. Nor that we should automatically

---

[117] Bessel Van Der Kolk, M.D., *The Body Keeps the Score: Brain, Mind, and Body in the Healing of Trauma* (New York: Penguin Books, 2014), 137, 174-175
[118] Ibid., 206.
[119] Ibid., 100.

give credence to every whispered rumor we hear. My point is that we must grasp the reality of how many among us have been hurt in this way, even when we're unable to talk about it—and that those who do open up about abuse are often suspected of lying because the stories seem disjointed, or the emotions don't line up with what one might expect.

Only after we have absorbed these realities and all they entail are we in the position to move on to the next step. Not that any of us are truly looking forward to doing so—but we must not let that stop us. While none but a sociopath would take pleasure in thinking about abuse—much less talking about these realities—we must consider that there are those among us who don't have the luxury of not thinking about what happened to them.

If we're not willing to educate ourselves and talk openly about these matters, we all have a lot to lose.

The Irony

Here's the irony of learning about others' deep pain. You will wish you could go back to the time before you knew about any of it. The worst I had ever dealt with was harassment, and I thought that was bad. I had no idea what others were going through. The less I understood the grim reality of sexual abuse, and the more naïve I was, the more I enjoyed life. However, though I was blissfully unaware, as the saying goes, that bliss came at a cost to those around me who needed love and care.

If those of us with less awareness don't genuinely absorb the enormity and sheer reality of pervasive sex crimes and abuse, we are not in the right position to understand, befriend, come alongside, love, and advocate for others in a way that takes into account their sexual selves.

Caring for Our Sexual Selves

First, let's consider those who have been harmed sexually. If we fail to take this aspect of humanity into account as mentors, Bible teachers, pastors, or leaders, we will miss key growth moments or biblical applications. As someone who's taught women's Bible studies and mentored Christian women over the years, I think of the way I've approached and sometimes avoided certain topics, and I cringe. Countless opportunities were lost. While I cannot go back, I can repent and go forward, forging a new and more constructive path.

One thing I know is that now that I'm aware of all I've missed, I'm unable to stay comfortable in that position any longer. Too much is at stake. When we avoid shining light on tough topics like sexual abuse, we lose the chance to confront abusers and call them to repentance. We also miss opportunities to comfort those who have been harmed sexually and encourage them along their healing process. In nearly all cases, this would involve connecting them to sympathetic and well-trained professionals who are specifically equipped to care for them in the ways that they most need.

We Are Not Okay

I don't know any woman who hasn't been harassed in some way, and although you may not be aware of it, you know a woman who's been raped. Statistics indicate that you likely know more than one, in fact.[120] Remember, one out of every six women has been the victim of an attempted or completed rape. Think of how many women you know and do the math. Then sit with that truth for a second.

Just because you're unaware of who these women are, that doesn't mean they're doing just fine. Long after the physical scars of a rape have healed, the mental, emotional, and spiritual fallout continues.

- 94% of women who are raped experience symptoms of post-traumatic stress disorder (PTSD) during the two weeks following the rape.
- 30% of women report symptoms of PTSD nine months after the rape.
- 33% of women who are raped contemplate suicide.
- 13% of women who are raped attempt suicide.
- Approximately 70% of rape or sexual assault victims experience moderate to severe distress, a larger

---

[120] As I have already pointed out, men also experience rape, and the experience is no less traumatizing for them. Since these cases are rarer, however, I'll be focusing largely here on how this affects women.

percentage than for any other violent crime.[121]

Rape and sexual assault are incredibly traumatic, and the fallout can prove soul-destroying. Those of us who have not experienced this particular violation, even while fully loving and caring for those who have, are ill-suited to meet the deep needs such trauma evokes. In fact, our well-meaning advice may just further the trauma. Cultivating connections to trained and trusted specialists is key.

We're Not Comfortable Disclosing

Sexual abuse, sexual assault, and rape all leave lasting scars on the psyche, yet the barriers to disclosing are high.

- Will anyone believe me?
- Will they think it's my fault?
- Will people see me the same way after they find out?
- Will speaking up ruin people's lives?
- Will I have to explain all the details?

If someone was abused in the past or when they were young, there are additional barriers to coming forward.

---

[121] Rape, Abuse & Incest National Network (RAINN), "Victims of Sexual Violence: Statistics," https://www.rainn.org/statistics/victims-sexual-violence (Accessed June 6, 2020).

- Will people think I'm making it up?
- Will they wonder why I waited so long?
- Would it be better if I just keep quiet and let the past stay in the past?

These are very real concerns. If the only time people hear us talking about sexual abuse or assault is when we're swapping theories over high-profile cases and celebrity accusations, those who have been abused may hear what we say and apply it to themselves.

"If they don't believe her, they wouldn't believe me." And the cycle of silence continues.

Breaking Our Silence

Scripture records multiple rapes. One of them is in 2 Samuel 13, in which we read the account of Amnon and Tamar. Amnon, a son of King David, is said to love his sister Tamar. He lies down in his room, pretending to be ill, and asks for her to be sent to cook for him and feed him. When he has her alone, he first propositions her. He takes hold of her and says, "Come lie with me, my sister."

Deeply disadvantaged in this situation, Tamar nevertheless advocates for herself. But Amnon would not listen to her, and Scripture records that "being stronger than she," he rapes her. Afterward, he throws her out of his chamber and bolts the door. Tamar puts ashes on her head (a sign of mourning) and tears the long-sleeved robe that she wears (a garment symbolic of her status as a virgin daughter). Hands to her head, torn sleeves trailing behind her, Tamar departs from Amnon's room, crying aloud.

She travels from Amnon's rooms crying and lamenting until she reaches her brother Absalom. However far a distance that was, no one responds to her lament or steps in to advocate for her. People would have seen the undeniable cultural symbols and recognized that something happened, but no one stepped in or got involved. This is a problem in and of itself. But when Tamar reaches her brother Absalom's residence, the first words out of his mouth are this: "Has your brother Amnon been with you?"

Not "What happened?" Not "Who did this to you?"

But "Has your brother Amnon been with you?"

This speaks volumes to Amnon's reputation, and the open awareness Absalom has of Amnon's intentions and what he's capable of. What happens next is not in any way a proper model for handling sexual abuse, but we have to give Absalom credit for believing Tamar and actually naming her abuser. Some fail to do even that.

Calling Them Out

In February of 2019, the *Houston Chronicle* launched a six-part series titled "Abuse of Faith," in which a team of journalists details twenty years' worth of sexual abuse cases in the Southern Baptist Convention (SBC). While this isn't the only Christian denomination to grapple with the reality of sexual abusers in their ranks, the SBC is currently the largest Protestant denomination in the United States. As such, the particulars of this investigation are worth noting.

The findings in the report are chilling.

- Pastors, employees, and volunteers who exhibited predatory behavior were still able to find jobs.

- In some cases, church leaders failed to alert law enforcement about complaints or to warn other congregations about allegations of misconduct.

- Past presidents and prominent leaders of the Southern Baptist Convention are among those criticized by victims for concealing or mishandling abuse complaints within their own churches or seminaries.

- Some registered sex offenders returned to the pulpit. Others remain there.

- Many of the victims were adolescents who were molested, sent explicit photos or texts, exposed to pornography, photographed nude, or repeatedly raped by youth pastors.

- Some victims as young as three years old were molested or raped inside pastors' studies and Sunday school classrooms. A few were adults—women and men who sought pastoral guidance and instead say they were seduced or sexually assaulted.[122]

---

[122] Robert Downen, Lise Olsen, and John Tedesco. "Abuse of Faith: 20 Years, 700 Victims: Southern Baptist sexual abuse spreads as leaders resist reforms." *Houston Chronicle.* https://www.houstonchronicle.com/news/investigations/article/Southern-Baptist-sexual-abuse-spreads-as-leaders-13588038.php?converted=1 (Accessed April 30, 2021).

Though in some instances abusers were named, turned in, prosecuted, and punished by law, in many cases they were not.

David Pittman was only twelve years old, he says, when a youth minister from his Georgia church first molested him in 1981. Two other former members of the man's churches said in interviews that they also were abused by this minister. But by the time Pittman spoke out in 2006, it was too late to press criminal charges. The minister still works at an SBC church.[123]

After pointing out that churches in the Southern Baptist Convention are particularly susceptible to abuse because they have a high level of autonomy, the reporters outline how victims have been abandoned, shunned, and shamed into silence. Repeatedly through the six-part *Houston Chronicle* series, a pattern emerges. When contacted for their sides of the stories, the organizations that mishandled abuse claims, the abusers themselves, and the churches that employed them either fail to respond to requests for interviews or decline to comment. As if refusing to talk about the events can make them go away.

Loss and Gain

A few weeks ago, I was chatting with a college student about the tendency in some circles to try to hide shameful stories like sex abuse scandals. She'd noticed a pattern to sweep things under the rug, not talk about the issues, pretend nothing ever happened. "I mean, I guess they want to protect God's reputation," she told me.

---

[123] Ibid.

"To protect all the good things the ministry is doing. They don't want people hearing about Christians doing bad things because that would harm the witness."

It's a line of thinking most of us have heard before. But it's entirely backwards. We cannot, in any way, harm God or his reputation. He sits in the heavens, forever enthroned in glory. Nothing we can or ever will do threatens one ounce of his worth or honor. We can, however, lose our own earthly reputations and tarnish the image of our little self-made kingdoms. It is not God the silencers are protecting.

Furthermore, as a just God, Yahweh desires to see justice done on earth. We know this not only because he tells us this about himself directly in Scripture but because he shows us this aspect of his nature in the way he behaves. He is forever bringing sin into the light where it can be atoned for, mended, and healed. We see this pattern established all the way back in the Garden of Eden. After the Fall, God doesn't wait for Adam and Eve to come to him. When they try to hide what they've done, he goes to seek them out himself, calling them by name and prompting them to bring their sin into the light of his presence. If we were truly concerned with maintaining a reflection of his character to a watching world, we would act as God would act. Instead of hiding moral failings, covering up abuse, or sweeping it under the rug, we would bring it into the light. That would truly serve as a witness to a watching world, particularly in cases of sexual abuse and assault, incest and rape.

In writing to the Ephesian Christians, Paul admonishes them to "Take no part in the unfruitful works of darkness, but instead expose them . . . when anything is exposed by the light, it becomes visible, for anything that becomes visible is light . . . Look carefully then how you walk, not as unwise but as wise, making the best use of the time, because the days are evil."[124] While we should never discuss these matters in a gossipy way or to derive vicarious enjoyment through discussing them, it's vital that we shine the light of Christ's truth far and wide, exposing the evils of the world so they can be made right.

Beyond making abuse allegations public and openly seeking justice, we must also be aware of abuse victims in our midst. We can't assume no one is hurting simply because we've never heard them speak of it. Bear in mind that only 38% of child sex abuse victims ever disclose their abuse.[125] When we remember that it's likely our peer group includes victims of sex crimes, we will consider how we talk about abuse, prepare our children to face potential abuse, and preach and teach differently as a result.

Consider Our Comments

A few years ago, a very public sex-abuse scandal dominated the news cycle. As I was walking through a public place one weekend, I overheard one man say to another, "If she didn't speak up then, she has no business speaking up now." his tone was sharp, biting, dismissive. Absolutely devoid of any hint of sympathy.

---

[124] Ephesians 5:11-16.
[125] "Darkness to Light: Child Sex Abuse Statistics." *D2l.org.* https://www.d2l.org/wp-content/uploads/2017/01/all_statistics_20150619.pdf (Accessed April 30, 2021).

Although I hadn't heard the entire conversation, his comment seemed to communicate that it didn't even matter to him whether or not the allegations were true. What mattered was the timing of the disclosure, which I understood he assumed was being manipulated for political leverage.

As someone who had recently been walking with a sister in Christ through a disclosure of her own childhood sexual abuse, I had to overcome an immediate urge to physically accost this man. The desire to smack him in the face and publicly harangue him was so strong I actually went and locked myself in a bathroom until I had regained control. Once I had calmed down, my first prayer was to thank God that I had been the one walking by, not her. I could not begin to imagine the toll that comment would have had on her, particularly at that stage of her trauma recovery.

When we discuss abuse in public, we must remember that for many among us, abuse is not a hypothetical. It cannot and should not be discussed flippantly.

Prepare Our Children

As we learned in Chapter 4, if parents are hesitant to talk to their children about sex in the first place, we can only imagine how much higher the resistance to talking candidly with their children about sexual abuse and rape. However, given the stark realities, parents should be adding sexual safety to the list of other safety topics they cover as children are growing up. Nearly all children know to Stop, Drop, and Roll; but how many know what to do if someone touches them inappropriately? It's much more likely children will be sexually abused than catch fire.

Preparing our children and giving them tools for protection and language to advocate for themselves may feel awkward in the moment, but we must move past our own discomfort to protect them from the threat of real harm down the road.

Preach and Teach Differently

One of the best and most thoughtful sermons on Amnon's rape of Tamar that I've heard came from Dr. Eric Mason at Epiphany Fellowship in Philadelphia, Pennsylvania. In a sermon from April 29, 2018, Dr. Mason speaks hard truths on how families deal or don't deal with sexual trauma. Walking slowly and carefully through the passage, he discusses issues relating to consent, harassment, molestation, coercion, boundaries, incest, and rape.

At one point, while praising Tamar for her response to Amnon's advances, Dr. Mason says, "I love her fight. But this is not to say that if you balled up and couldn't fight, that it was still your fault. I just want to tell you in the text how she fought back."

With these carefully chosen comments, Dr. Mason speaks directly to rape victims, affirming and comforting them in what is likely an emotionally distressful moment of the sermon. He goes on to assure those who couldn't fight back that "Compliance to preserve personal safety . . . is still rape . . . That's covered in the Scriptures as well."[126]

---

[126] Dr. Eric Mason. "#MeToo." *Epiphany Fellowship Podcast.* https://podbay.fm/p/epiphany-fellowship-podcast/e/1525030769 (Accessed April 30, 2021).

That and much more is covered in Scriptures—which, as we know, are sufficient for every human need. Silence, family secrets, muzzling victims, inaction in the face of rape and sexual abuse—all these are recorded in Scriptural narratives for our observation and edification. Are we as willing to dive into these passages and excavate practical truth and application as we are the Psalms, the Gospels, and the book of James? When we remember that there are real abuse victims among us, we will preach and teach differently. Rather than avoiding hard passages, we will study them for the truths God embedded there for us.

What to Say

It's not easy to know how to respond when someone tells us they've been sexually abused or assaulted. If we're not prepared ahead of time, we can do very real damage with our knee-jerk reactions. According to the Rape, Abuse, and Incest National Network (RAINN), if someone does disclose sexual assault or abuse to you, listening without judgment is the first step to supporting a survivor. Believing someone, telling them they're not alone, that it's not their fault, and acknowledging that this experience has been painful are foundational first responses.

Support also means educating yourself ahead of time about access to resources, such as knowing how to reach the National Sexual Assault Hotline, how to seek medical attention, and how to report the crime to the police.[127]

Why It Matters

Sexual assault is associated with an increased lifetime rate of attempted suicide. In women in particular, a history of sexual trauma before age sixteen is an especially strong correlate of attempted suicide.[128] If for no other reason than this, these matters require our deep care, concern, and focused preparation. We cannot afford to bury our heads in the sand. Learning how to talk about these matters, learning how to create a culture in which survivors can come forward, receive love and care, and access the help they need to heal, means the difference between life and death.

Everything to Gain

Evil thrives in darkness yet flees when exposed to the light. When we're willing to press through discomfort to engage socially awkward conversations regarding sexual abuse and related trauma, we have everything to gain.

---

[127] Rape, Abuse & Incest National Network (RAINN), "Tips for Talking with Survivors of Sexual Assault," https://www.rainn.org/articles/tips-talking-survivors-sexual-assault (Accessed June 7, 2021).
[128] Davidson JRT, Hughes DC, George LK, Blazer DG. The Association of Sexual Assault and Attempted Suicide Within the Community. Arch Gen Psychiatry. 1996;53(6):550–555. doi:10.1001/archpsyc.1996.01830060096013

We are in a better position to:

- Bring sexual abusers into the light of God's justice
- Demonstrate compassion to the abuse victims in our midst
- Create safe and welcoming environments in which victims can disclose past abuse and seek justice and healing without fear of not being believed
- Educate our children and teach them tools to protect themselves against potential abuse
- Mine the whole counsel of Scripture for truth

May we find the rewards worth the risk.

Start Your Own Awkward Conversation

Find some trusted conversation partners for discussion or consider the questions on your own.

1. If someone were to disclose sexual abuse or rape, would you be likely to believe them or not believe them? Why is that the case?

2. In your experience, how have passages of Scripture detailing rapes been taught?

3. Would you say you are equipped to deal with disclosures

of molestation, sexual abuse, rape, and/or sexual trauma? What can you do to become more equipped?

4. What do we lose when we fail to press through discomfort and engage tough topics related to sexual abuse? What could we potentially gain by doing so?

Socially Awkward

Welcome to Awkwardsville
When You Need to Go

A few Octobers ago, my sister Bethany and I drove from Florida to South Carolina to visit our niece. We spent a long weekend with her, hiking among falling leaves, drinking coffees, and shooting the late-autumn breeze. As Floridians, we felt this was important. We don't really get seasons in Florida. Unless you count Hurricane Season.

I almost made it through the entire trip without an incident. Then, on Sunday afternoon, just a few hours before we departed, it happened.

We'd been staying with some local friends in the area, and after church, we joined them for lunch with some of their extended family. Since I'd been friends with Hilary and Jacob for over twenty years and had, in fact, been in their wedding, I knew most of their relatives, either on sight or by reputation. They also knew me, but not well at that point. We were definitely friends-of-friends tagging along and crashing lunch.

The meal was hosted by Hilary's sister-in-law Addy, who lives with her husband Dan and their children in a lovely, well-appointed home with bay windows and gorgeous views.

At some point, I needed to use the restroom. As one does. Having earlier spied what looked like a small powder room adjacent to the front door, I excused myself and slipped away. For all the size and weight of the large wooden door, it closed quietly, clicking shut with a soft snick. I quickly took care of business, washed my hands, and turned to exit. Only when I pushed down on the handle, the door wouldn't budge.

I jiggled the handle. Pushed, pulled, and tried to turn it. Nothing. How odd. Was I somehow doing it wrong? Nonsense. I'd been using doors my whole life.

And so began my nightmare.

I was trapped—out of sight and mind in a thick-walled, heavily-doored pocket bathroom with no phone. There was a small window, but it would have proven a challenge for my hips. I had visions of getting stuck, halfway in and halfway out, only to be noticed hours later by neighbors. The fire department would be called, and I would have to be cut out. It would make the evening news. Worse still, I'd never be able to compensate them for the property damage.

What to do, what to do.

I could bang on the door, of course. I could yell. Tap out "h.e.l.p.m.e." in Morse Code. While better than getting stuck in the window, the first two options felt beneath my dignity and the third was impossible. Why had I never learned Morse Code?

I swiped a hand across my forehead. Despite the chill in the late-October air, I was now sweating. Trust me, you would be, too.

I leaned my head against the heavy wooden door. From the

other side came a tap. Someone was knocking on the bathroom door from the outside! I was saved!

"Hello?" It was Dan, the homeowner.

"Yes!" I shrilled. "I'm here!'

"Are you . . . locked in?"

Imagine if I wasn't. Imagine if I were just . . . taking a long time. How embarrassing.

"Yes," I said. "But I don't know how this happened."

It happened because the door was an antique, with an equally antique locking mechanism. This was information I would only learn later, you understand. This was no time for a history lesson.

"You have to run your hand underneath," Dan explained. "There's a little catch. Do you feel it?"

I did. Heaving a sigh, I pulled the door open and stepped out.

That's when I saw the welcome committee.

At some point, as the host had come to rescue me, the entire group had gathered outside the bathroom. They'd arranged themselves in double lines facing one another, arms lifted overhead, hands clasped in the center to make an arch, cheering to welcome my egress.

To this day, none of the adults can remember whose idea the arch was. Rather than trying to point fingers at one another, however, the rest of the group all seem convinced in their own minds that it was their idea. The only person we've been able to rule out for sure is Bethany, who—in her own words—was "over by the fireplace minding my own business."

By my estimation, it seems to have been the spontaneous decision of a group that, for one glorious moment in time, is perfectly in sync. Everyone makes eye contact and somehow instantly knows what the other is thinking.

"What if we—"

"Should we?"

"Of course!"

"Let's go!"

The chairs shove back, and there's a mad scramble. The adults snap their fingers and hiss at the children, who are confused, but excited to be involved. There's stifled laughter, socks sliding on the hardwood floor, and plenty of shushing. Everyone falls into place, hands locked, just as the door springs open.

But of course, I'm just guessing. What would I know?

I was locked in the bathroom the entire time.

CHAPTER 12
Pressing Forward

This book is titled *Socially Awkward* for a reason. If we take seriously the call to embrace discomfort for the sake of others, we'll be going against the flow—both of general society and perhaps even our own Christian subculture. And going against the flow comes with risks.

The Risks Involved

Throughout the book, I've gone out of my way to highlight the risks involved when we fail to press through discomfort to engage though topics. But I don't want to present an idealized view of what can happen when we embrace the awkward and insist on having hard conversations. Speaking out comes with a cost.

If you're in a position of influence, you could lose favor with those who have real power to remove you from your position—or at least threaten to do so if you don't stop bringing up awkward and uncomfortable topics. You could lose supporters and donors. Even without an obvious leadership position or influencer label, we are all embedded in a complex web of families, social groups, and faith communities. These are the most important relationships in our lives. To risk losing our place is to risk losing everything.

And it is a risk. Having awkward conversations is a messy business, and there's danger in romanticizing the process. It can result in some very real losses. Even though I wrote this entire book, I still don't relish bringing up hard and awkward conversations around serious and polarizing issues. I don't particularly enjoy acting as the "Well Actually" Girl. I'd much rather talk about books and movies and where you're headed on your next vacation.

Yet I've come to recognize the harm that is perpetuated when we fail to talk about hard things; and given what we have to lose versus what we could potentially gain by engaging in more open and honest dialogue, I've found the risk to be worth the reward. When I become weary and discouraged, I come back to the underlying purpose that drives me. When I remember why I do this in the first place, I am often freshly motivated to move forward in love.

In doing so over the years, I've also gained some hard-won wisdom. I'd like to conclude by sharing some of it with you.

Ruth's Rules for Engaging Tough Topics

Rule 1: The medium matters.

The more awkward the topic, the more many of us tend to avoid face-to-face confrontations on the matter. We want to confess past sins in a long letter, admit we were wrong over the phone, break up with someone via text. We want to argue online, behind the safety of a screen. But these are not the most helpful paths forward.

In general, the tougher the topic is going to be, the more important it is that you favor direct, person-to-person communication. We can more completely share our views and learn from direct conversation partners. Not only do the words we speak matter, but body language and tone of voice play vital roles in completing any connection.

In the 1970s, Iranian-born psychology professor Albert Mehrabian conducted studies on communication and determined that effective face-to-face exchange of emotions or attitudes can be broken down into three key categories: nonverbal behavior (facial expressions, for example), tone of voice, and the literal meaning of the spoken word.[129]

According to Mehrabian's rule, whether we like a person will depend largely on these three elements being in congruence when a person puts forward a message concerning their feelings. Their facial expressions account for 55% of our opinion, their tone of voice for 38%, and their words for only 7%. If, for instance, someone takes a bite of a pie you've made and wheezes, "Oh, yes, this is delicious" while simultaneously grimacing heavily and fanning themselves with a free hand, the tone of voice and the nonverbal clues will carry more weight with you than their words, which come across in this context as an obvious lie.

That's because we instinctively understand what Mehrabian's

---

[129] British Library, "Albert Mehrabian," https://www.bl.uk/people/albert-mehrabian# (Accessed January 22, 2021).

rule so effectively summarizes: that for effective communication involving our emotions to take place, these three legs of the communication tripod need to be in complete alignment. When they are not, we're able to spot the difference. When they line up, however, we're able to communicate with complete sincerity and form bonds of trust. Even if people might disagree with us on principle, when our words, actions, and tone of voice all communicate the same message, they're able to determine whether we're acting in good faith.

That's why when difficult matters must be discussed, they're best discussed face-to-face.

Rule 2: Context matters.

One thing I love about Jesus is the different ways in which he responds to those who approach him. To the weak and broken, he is gentle and forthcoming. To the proud and aggressive, he's abrupt and sometimes even purposefully opaque.

How you decide to go about engaging these tough topics depends not just on you and your baseline personality but also on the context of those with whom you're talking. Some circumstances certainly call for a battering ram. Others require a key. Still others only call for a gentle touch of the hand for the door to swing wide open. If you are unsure which method will work best, ask for guidance in prayer.

The person to whom you're speaking matters. The nature of the conversation matters. The subject matters. Learn from the wisdom of Jesus in this regard and respond appropriately.

Rule 3: Disagreement does not create enemies.

When talking about tough topics, it's no surprise that things can get heated. Blood pressure rises, emotions balloon, tempers flare. When I speak up and others dissent, I must constantly remind myself that A) in some cases, I still might be wrong, and that B) even when I'm right, my fight is not with the people in front of me but with the false idea that they hold.

If you hear nothing else I've said in this book, please hear this. You only have one true enemy, and that is *the* enemy—Satan. Anything that flows from him, therefore, is also your enemy. Lies are your enemy. Hatred is your enemy. Strife is your enemy. Fear is your enemy. Delusions are your enemy. Ignorance is your enemy. False narratives are your enemy.

The people with whom you hold these hard discussions are not your enemies. They are sisters and brothers whom you're called to serve.

Those opposing truth are victims of Satan and his lies. This is where we all start. Remember, no one springs fully formed from Zeus's helmet like Athena did, full of all wisdom and knowledge. Rather, we come to faith as little children. We are sheep gone astray. Little lambs who follow the Lamb of God. We've been brought out of darkness into the Kingdom of Christ's marvelous light.

Whether your conversation partner is a fellow Christ-follower or not, you would do well to meditate on your own journey and remember that there was a time you knew none of what you know now. In fact, you are still on a journey and have not yet arrived at the pinnacle of wisdom.

In one way or another, we are all in constant need of liberation. "You will know the truth," Jesus tells us, "and the truth will set you free."[130] That is our prayer. Not that we will be proven right and the other person wrong. Not that we will win, and they will lose. But that together we will be able to stand side by side, beholding the truth and walking in its light.

Rule 4: Conversations work best in a series.

Our deepest and most effective conversations will take place in the context of relationships and span many years. Instead of being a one-and-done, drive-through event, deep conversations about tough topics can be lengthy, punctuated affairs that unspool over a matter of weeks, months, and years. Despite the energy and care required, these will prove some of the best conversations of your life.

When taking the long view, you don't have to put all the pressure of getting everything right—saying everything you've ever thought or felt—during one coffee date. Instead, you both can marinate, learn, wrestle, and grow together. Some of these conversations, and the friendships they're formed around, will eventually go with us into the New Kingdom. Except then, on that day, instead of knowing in part, we'll know and understand in full, even as we are now fully known and fully loved by an all-seeing, all-knowing, and ever-loving God.

All will be made right.

And nothing will be awkward.

---

[130] John 8:32.

Start Your Own Awkward Conversation

Find some trusted conversation partners for discussion or consider the questions on your own.

1. Over the course of reading this book, how have your perspectives on socially awkward conversations changed?

2. When it comes to talking about tough topics, which of your preconceived notions have been affirmed? Which have been discounted?

3. What are the potential dangers of talking about hard things with friends, family members, and loved ones— particularly in relationships that already bear long-standing patterns of avoidance?

4. Why is it worth it to press through discomfort to engage tough topics?

Socially Awkward

Acknowledgments

To Bethany and Jodee: You know the extent of how awkward I am and love me in spite of it (and, at times, try to gently love me out of it). You were early conversation partners on the bulk of these topics. This book would not exist without all our talks.

To the Socially Awkward Beta Reading Team: Brandy Anderson, Laura Russell Hughes, Hilary Forrest, Josh Headrick, Sarah Malone, Naomi Pagan, and Lucy Crabtree. You asked hard questions, pushed for clarity, deliberated, and confirmed. This book is stronger because of your investment. Thank you.

Nathan and Dawn: For giving me space to write in the cabin in the woods. Never mind about the bees.

To the carpenter bees who swarmed the cabin the entire time I worked on this draft: for inspiring me with their driving force, boundless energy, and dramatic insistence. You made so much noise that I found it impossible to ignore you. May we all take a lesson from you.

To the God who made the bees—and who also made me, thank you.

About the Author

Ruth Buchanan is a Christian writer who holds degrees in ministry and theology. She's traditionally published in the areas of fiction, non-fiction, plays, and sacred scripts. Though usually clamped to the keyboard, Ruth is also an eager reader, an enthusiastic traveler, and the world's most reluctant runner. She serves as Director of Literary Services for Build a Better Us.

Also by the Author

Every week across this country, single members filter into their local congregations to worship, minister, and serve with their brothers and sisters in Christ. Although a minority in most congregations, singles compose a strong cross-section of the church body. Each blessed and challenged with individual circumstances, Christian singles not only bear a unique burden but also offer diverse perspectives on the Christian life. Unfortunately, many Christian singles attest to feeling overlooked. Pastors and church leaders, many long married, often

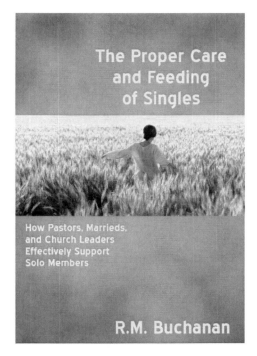

find themselves ill-equipped to understand the particular relational, emotional, and spiritual needs of long-term Christian singles. Worse, they're unaware that they're underequipped. Married church members, though sympathetic to the needs of their single friends, nevertheless struggle to bridge the divide. Written by a dedicated Christ-follower and long-term Christian single, The Proper Care and Feeding of Singles addresses the issues with humor and grace, offering practical solutions to strengthen the bonds of love and fellowship within local congregations.

Also by Entrusted Books

Bible Studies

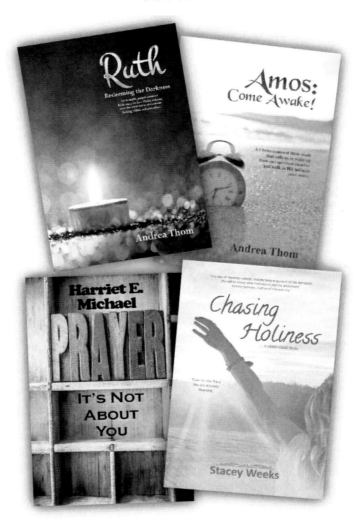

Devotionals

Socially Awkward

Thank you
for reading our books.

If you enjoyed this inspirational book,
please consider returning to its
purchase page and leaving a review.

Look for other books
published by

E

Entrusted Books
an Imprint of
Write Integrity Press, LLC

www.WriteIntegrity.com

Made in United States
North Haven, CT
14 March 2022

17071628R00139